HANDBOOK FOR PIANO PRACTICE

A guide to life-long learning in music through continuing education in piano

For students and teachers

Victoria B. Stearns

William R. Parks
WParksPublishing@aol.com

www.wrparks.com

Dedication:
In memory of my teachers
Carol Hoffman Juette
Livingston Gearhart
Leo Smit

And to all piano students and their teachers

Copyright © 2014 by Victoria B. Stearns

ISBN: 978-0-88493-018-1

Library of Congress Control Number: 2014913671

MUSIC
The greatest good that mortals know
And all of Heaven we have below

Joseph Addison
A Song for St Cecilia's Day

The best way to learn about a work of music is to play it
Charles Rosen
Piano Notes

TABLE OF CONTENTS

Introduction: this is a guide, not a "method"   7
The "older" student   9
      Encouragement and advice
Getting started   11
      Historical note about pianos
      Choosing an instrument
      Where to place your piano
      Seating
      Lighting
      Eyeglasses
      Piano maintenance, cleaning, tuning
      Finding a teacher
      Length and frequency of lessons, and a note on etiquette
The first lesson   16
      Sitting at the piano
      Hand position
      Fingers
      Note reading
      Rhythm
      Summary: reaping the musical benefits
Your musical library: 22
      First items to purchase, give up "methods" as quickly as possible, recommended materials, including a music dictionary, real piano literature, also a word about photocopying, CD's, and recording

The first six months: making progress, tips for technique, exercises, scales, reinforcing what you have learned   25

Learning a new piece of music: overview: key factors to look for, and the three things to tackle first (correct pitch, rhythm, and workable fingering)   28

Adult restarters: how to get back in shape, retrieve and reinforce what you already know, laying groundwork for a solid foundation, choosing repertoire   31
Rhythm: pianists often have rhythm problems due to the lack of group experience. Here are detailed tips that truly work, if heeded. The importance of rests.   34

Basic Training: Bach. Why Bach is so important. Bach wrote simple pieces for early learners. Advantages of learning his works. How you will be training your eyes and ears without actually realizing it. The study of Bach provides the key to learning virtually any music written. Explanation of opus numbers, BWV, K, etc.   36

Approaching a new piece of music: now more details are given.   39
Phrasing, articulation, interpretation. The importance of sight reading.

The Pedals. Pedaling needs its own page (it is mentioned in the previous chapter).
Directions are simplified and much of the mystique explained.   42

Tips for good practice habits. This section can be revisited and reviewed at any level, as poor practice habits are the biggest time-waster and lead to a lack of progress, which in turn engenders discouragement and even quitting.   44

Fine-tuning your playing. How to make your playing more accurate, sound more "musical" and in the proper style. This section should also be restudied.   46

Memorization. In general, concert and recital performances are beyond the scope of this book. Here, suggestions for memory work are given. 48

Sight Reading. More tips and information, ideas of what to use for material.   49

Popular Music and Jazz. Some introductory comments on how to get started.   50

Introduction to Piano Literature: the basic periods with stylistic principles are listed, followed by chronological lists of literature. A detailed Sample Syllabus of Literature is included, for specific choices of works at the elementary through upper intermediate/early advanced (graded "levels" vary so much it is impossible to give exact numbers) 52

Scale Practice   67

Explanation of Sonata Form   69

Book List   71

We are in an age of transition, but it is still highly useful to have a few references at hand. Herewith, a few recommendations for dictionaries, books on learning more about music, music history, and appreciation. References for teachers are included.

In conclusion, a few "good reads" about pianists, pianos, and music. Learning the piano should encompass the whole world of music, the doors of which should now be open. Fiction and movies with musical themes should become more enjoyable and understandable.

Theory   74

Half and whole steps
Intervals
Triads
Inversions
Basic arpeggio
Major scales
Circle of 5ths (beginning)
Triads built on the degrees of the scale
Minor scales
Adding minor scales to the circle of 5ths
Getting familiar with the concept of "key"; transposing a simple tune
What is harmony?
Hearing a progression (beginning with V-I)
Cadences
Brief introduction to 7th chords (dominant 7th and diminished 7th)
Complete Circle of 5ths

INTRODUCTION

The presence of a piano breathes life into a room in a way nothing else can. It is silently understood that music is played here. The instrument beckons.

A century ago, the piano was a fixture in the average home. A great many people learned to play, not only the basic piano literature, but also arrangements of symphonies, chamber music, operas. Without sound recordings, the only way to hear the older classics or the latest "hits" was to play them yourself. We are not speaking of conservatory training for concert performers here, but of ordinary people making music.

The performance of music has somehow garnered an aura of extreme difficulty and striving for perfection. These feelings might also be held about sports, yet many people enjoy playing golf or tennis without being intimidated by the superstars. If it is possible to enjoy biking without qualifying for the Tour de France, then it should be the same with music. Music has the additional advantage that you can constantly improve throughout your life plus build on your basic knowledge.

Practice, practice, practice. Yes, learning the piano takes time and effort. But it is not impossibly difficult, and is well within the range of the majority of people. *How* you practice determines your progress. If you learn to practice efficiently, getting the maximum benefits for the time spent, progress will be readily apparent. As one who learned the hard way, I can assure you that it is quite possible to save literally hundreds of wasted hours.

The purpose of this book is to show you how. Piano lessons can serve several purposes and have many side benefits, much needed in today's society: reducing stress, keeping the brain active by learning a new skill, bringing sanity and tranquility into a world supercharged with speed and technology. Quite simply, it would be a much better world if more people played music. Lessons can also be a springboard to music appreciation: if you learn the theme of *Ode to Joy* at your first lesson, hopefully you will also learn something about Beethoven.

This book is a companion and guide, not a lesson by lesson manual, but giving encouragement to get over the "hump" to the next level of ability, and to make the most of your time. You may wish to reread some of the advice when you have advanced to different stages.

Dip into the sections that are pertinent at the moment. Commentary obviously aimed at beginners may be useful for teachers or piano pedagogy students. Teachers are limited by the time constraints of the piano lesson, and often do not have the time for detailed explanations.

The process is a continuous one, life-long learning that can be mind-expanding, deepening, enriching, and rewarding at every level, a connection with the greatest composers of music.

The journey has begun.

THE "OLDER" STUDENT

This book is for *all* piano students and their teachers, with a certain emphasis on guiding older students. As the principles of good playing are the same for everyone, much of the material will be useful for teachers of younger children.

"Nothing is quite so demanding of a brain as musical performance, which involves the choreography of hundreds of muscles, eyes moving across instrument and score, ears following every nuance, written symbols decoded and interpreted, several kinds of memory churning, emotions summoned and deployed, whole passages planned and administered, everything reciprocating to elicit a particular style, and all this without the various activities colliding. It's no wonder that it takes so long to learn an instrument well, and that truly great musicians are so rare."
Robert Jourdain, *Music, the Brain, and Ecstasy*, from the Introduction, xv.

Whew. The above is a lot to digest. Please be assured that it is much simpler just to *play*, much like the famous advice that Laurence Olivier gave to Dustin Hoffman, about merely *acting*....

Another book best left for later on, *Playing the Piano for Pleasure*, by Charles Cooke, has sound advice but is far too advanced, to the point of being intimidating, for beginning or intermediate students.

Equally disconcerting are books that promise that you can learn piano in a day. Well, you can learn some things, but real progress takes time. The important thing is to keep the thread going, don't give up, even if you have to miss several weeks of lessons for some unforeseen circumstances. Anyone who really wants to learn, can.

Lessons are not simply aimed at retirees. Younger adults can and do make time in their lives for music, which becomes an oasis from stresses they are facing. Finding time is the main concern. A twelve year old learns faster than an eight year old, but the eight year old has more time to build the habit of practice.

Please disregard anything you read about the optimal learning age of six (or younger). Yes, if you are aspiring to a professional or concert career.

But many, many older students have learned well, to a remarkable level, despite busy schedules, and have achieved understanding, appreciation, and enjoyment of music as active participants.

How much time is wasted continues to astound me: poor practice habits, poor sense of rhythm, errors in teaching (you don't learn "F" sharp, you learn what a sharp is). I have tried to compile all the pertinent material into the book I wish I had had as a student.

GETTING STARTED

HISTORICAL NOTE.

You will sometimes see the word *pianoforte*, which is the original name given to the instrument. Bartolomeo Cristofori of Florence, Italy, is credited with its invention, sometime in the first decade of the eighteenth century, the traditionally held date of 1709 now thought to be earlier. The instrument could play both soft (piano) and loud (forte) by the amount of pressure on the keys. Until then, harpsichord keys would not sound any louder if struck more forcefully, as the strings are plucked by jacks, and the sound of the clavichord was so weak that it could not be heard in the next room.

In today's age of technology and amplification, we cannot possibly fathom what a "big deal" this new instrument actually was. Some famous piano makers include Stein, Broadwood, Erard, and Steinway. A delightful book entitled *The Piano Shop on the Left Bank* (see reading list) includes history of the piano in a very readable manner.

CHOOSING AN INSTRUMENT.

In order to learn to play properly, please consider purchasing a real piano. There really is no substitute. Although prices of new grand pianos may seem astronomical, a good, serviceable upright can be acquired for a few hundred dollars. Some music stores will rent instruments. Tell the staff that you would like a firm action. There are sales at music stores, estate and moving sales. As a general rule, it is not wise to purchase an instrument that has had a great deal of use, such as from schools. It is definitely worth a professional technician's fee in appraising an instrument before purchase.

You can find a technician through the music store, music schools, concert halls (who tunes for concerts?) Some older uprights can be a real bargain, while others are too costly to fix and may be impossible to keep in tune.

Sizes (height in inches)
36 spinet
40 console
45 studio upright
48-50 upright

Some tips:
1. Ask the height of the piano, the make, and its age, if known.
2. Go and look at it, as a piece of furniture, and see if you like it.
3. Look at the condition of the keys, and inside, the condition of the felts on the hammers. Notice if they are deeply ridged (if they are too deeply ridged, the piano might not be able to be tuned properly, and may be too costly to fix)

A word about keyboards. Keyboards are portable, perhaps useful for theory assignments or composing, or in a situation where you need to work without disturbing others. They might be an economical way to ascertain whether or not a younger student is interested enough to keep taking lessons. After about six months, it is time to consider acquiring a piano, which can be far less costly that a state of the art keyboard. There are serious drawbacks to continue practicing on a keyboard:

Disorientation of finding the notes, which unfortunately increases rapidly as the range of the music increases. Some keyboards even have narrower keys, which is a further complication. Middle C is not in the center, except on 88 note keyboards.

Lack of finger strengthening, as it is too easy to play, so a proper "touch" is not developed. Even with weighted keys, the keyboard is still a machine; it is impossible to develop a clear and "singing" tone, degrees of touch and control, and to learn to listen to yourself. The sound, to my mind, is very "commercial" and cannot come even close to the beauty of a true piano sound. Lastly, it is very difficult to make the transition to a real piano. The piano is the counterpart of today's "slow food".

WHERE TO PLACE YOUR PIANO. What a decorator recommends might not be the best for your instrument. Avoid outside walls, windows, doorways (anywhere there might be continual drafts) excessive heat (fireplace) or possible water leaks. As little fluctuation in room temperature as possible is the best for the piano, with sufficient humidity. Larry Fine in *The Piano Book* (see Book List) suggests that the ideal temperature is 64 degrees with the humidity about 50%. Some areas have too much humidity, and a dehumidifier might be useful. In areas with severe winters, more humidity will be needed (houseplants can help this situation). To protect the finish and avoid spillage, do not place vases of flowers or potted plants on the piano.

SEATING.
Bench, stool, chair. The choice is yours: experiment. Stools and some benches are adjustable. I have always preferred a piano chair, for added back support.

LIGHTING.
Here again, there are many choices and styles: floor lamp, ceiling fixture, the so-called "piano lamp", or other table or desk size. Have the source of light on the left side. Some people need brighter lights than others.

EYEGLASSES.
You want to be able to read the music comfortably. If you have trouble seeing or focusing on the music, consult your eye physician. Older students who already have bifocals might consider the special glasses that are for middle distance only (many computer specialists use these also). Younger students should not be forgotten if they are having problems reading the notes: eyesight should be checked.

PIANO MAINTENANCE. Cleaning. A slightly damp cloth (water only) is all that is necessary to clean the keys. Pianos have been made with plastic keys for decades now, but if you have a much older piano, it may have ivory keys (you can tell by the color, and by the line on the key). Clean in the same way. For the piano case, other than dusting with a soft cloth, consult your technician. Cleaning inside the piano should be done prior to tuning. A two inch paint brush can be used to clean between the strings, then, vacuuming can be done.

Tuning. Regarding upkeep, a piano is not unlike a car, as they both require regular maintenance. Normally, a piano should be tuned at least twice a year (usually when the heat goes on or off for the season, but *not immediately*; it is best to wait a bit). More frequent tuning is needed if a piano is brand new, or hasn't been tuned in some time. Humidity and temperature (as well as playing) affect the tuning. A stable indoor temperature is generally preferable, with some increased humidity in a northern winter, and dehumidifying in climates where necessary.

Remember that the sound will be different in a living room with furniture, carpets, drapes, etc., when compared to the acoustics of a concert hall. Your tuner or technician can advise on the quality or "brilliance" of the sound.

The higher the pitch of the concert "A" will affect the brilliance, but the piano may fall out of tune sooner.

Basically, what you need is an instrument in decent enough tune so you can hear correctly. Every piano is different: your teacher's, the one at church or school, even two of the same model. A fascinating book, *Grand Obsession* (see reading list) is the story of one woman's quest for the perfect piano. Be sure to ask your technician's advice regarding such situations as long travels, closing up your home, moving. You always want professional piano movers to handle your instrument.

FINDING A TEACHER. Private lessons truly are the only way to learn smoothly; learning to listen (more about the importance of this will follow) without developing unsuitable habits or ingraining mistakes (improper hand position or technique). There really is no substitute for the one to one ratio. Group lessons can be too noisy, discouraging (if you don't get to play) or even counterproductive, if you do play but errors aren't corrected. If electronic instruments are used, you cannot learn the proper touch. Attempting to teach yourself from a book, without any instruction, will not be successful, and often with the same results as mentioned above.

What do you most want in a teacher? Qualifications, expertise, experience, willingness to help your personal goals and interests, personality? The best way to find a teacher is by personal reference, word of mouth, the same way you would search for a new doctor or any other professional. You can ask your piano technician (he tunes the teachers' instruments also), call local music schools or music departments, music stores, churches. Notice which names keep popping up. Keep in mind that the most brilliant performer is not necessarily the best teacher. One who has learned with some difficulty is better equipped to deal with ordinary problems.

Telephone the teachers on your list and ask questions such as "can you tell me something about your approach?" cost of lessons, policy on missed lessons. Some teachers have monthly rates. In this case, it might be advisable to ask for a brief meeting, or an interview, before signing up. If the teacher charges by the lesson, you could always try one lesson. You want a teacher you are comfortable with and have confidence in.

LENGTH AND FREQUENCY OF LESSONS. Beginners can manage for awhile with a well-packed half hour lesson. The ideal timing for lessons is once a week, but in today's world, that is not always possible. Students who are highly motivated and self-disciplined can make adequate progress with less frequent lessons, perhaps every other week, but the key issue is the motivation to practice. If practice doesn't happen, there won't be any progress, and the student will quickly become discouraged. There is the added problem of practicing errors longer. Once a student has reached an intermediate level, forty-five minutes to an hour will usually be needed. Lessons should be a form of continuing education, without long summer breaks; too much time off requires much reviewing and relearning in the fall.

A note on etiquette. Try to arrive promptly for your lessons. Find out your teacher's policy on missed lessons. If you have to miss a lesson, call as soon as possible; don't wait until the last minute for a non-emergency. If you decide to stop lessons, please do let your teacher know. A note can serve the purpose if telephoning seems too awkward. For students going off to college, your teacher would appreciate hearing from you.

Be honest if you haven't had much time to practice. Come for your lesson anyway. Rather than making excuses, the time can be spent much more profitably, on technique, sight reading, theory, and most important of all, actually learning a new piece, how to go about it, and how to practice it. There is so much material to be covered, which cannot always fit into the regular lesson.

Also, please rest assured that your teacher is very aware that you "played it better at home." Don't ever be afraid of making mistakes. The important point is to be able to recognize a mistake, and learn how to fix it.

Perfection is not the goal. Even the greatest artists have finger slips. Far more important is the ability to be able to work out a piece correctly on your own.

THE FIRST LESSON
(Absolute beginners)

For very young children, all that is really necessary at the first lesson is to learn that the music lesson is a comfortable, happy situation. Older children, teen-agers, and adults should learn a few basics, hopefully sparking the thirst for knowledge.

SITTING AT THE PIANO.
You want to be centered, opposite Middle C, at a comfortable distance for your arms and legs. Good posture is essential for maximum maneuverability and avoidance of tensed up muscles, leading to back, neck, and shoulder pain. Sit straight: to avoid slouching, think "shoulders below ears". Arms should be parallel to the floor when playing. Feet should be flat on the floor, ready to pedal if desired. Shoes should be as thin as possible (even slippers or simply socks). Sneakers are not recommended. This may seem like a tall order, but it will become automatic fairly quickly.

Should you find yourself tensing up, do some neck and shoulder rolls. Shake out arms and wrists, make a fist and relax it.

Remember to stay centered at Middle C. To play in both upper and lower ranges, your arms reach for the notes; you do not move your body. Your fingers will learn the location of the notes. The only time you are not centered is for playing duets, then Middle C is the divider between the players.

HAND POSITION.
Bracelets, bangles, and other accoutrements can actually harm the piano keys and case, as well as deter from flexibility, balance, and mobility. I myself find even a wristwatch too cumbersome, and remove it for playing, though some will disagree.

Please do not be concerned about the size or shape of your hands, or the length of your fingers. All sizes and shapes can play. Hand position should be a flatter wrist and palm, parallel to the keyboard, with *curved* fingers. No "holding" imaginary oranges or balls. I think this age-old suggestion was offered to deter young children from dropping their wrists, which seems to happen automatically. Watch close-ups of concert artists on television. You will notice a flatter palm, fingers close to the keys. This position aids a surer attack on the desired note. The less unnecessary movement, the better. Get in the habit of keeping your hands near the keyboard, ready to play.

It may feel "odd" to have your hands held in this manner, after all, they have done many tasks, but nothing quite like this. In a few weeks, you won't feel strange.

A word about fingernails. Yes, the shorter, the better, but you don't have to cut them immediately. It is indeed possible to play to a certain level with long fingernails. That said, long fingernails are the opposite of the ideal, which is a fingertip that you can actually feel interacting with the key. Dexterity, rapid passage work, and big chords do not work with long fingernails.

FINGERS.
Thumb is no. 1, index finger no. 2, and so on. As stated above, you need to play with curved fingers, which will take awhile to develop. Your fingers may seem uncooperative, shooting out in the wrong direction, but please be patient. Thumb and index finger are the strongest, and can easily overpower the other fingers. There are simple exercises to tone the remaining three, to achieve equality of strength, and for evenness of sound. Most probably, you will be given a five finger exercise on C at this lesson.

NOTE READING. The piano encompasses all the notes played by an orchestra. There are 88 keys, 52 white and 36 black. The musical alphabet consists of only seven letters, A-G. N.B. *Note reading is best learned directly, without gimmicks.* Read from the staff. Notes floating around without staff lines only lead to confusion. No color coding, pasting note names on the keys, or worse, writing them on the printed music, or reading notes by finger numbers, such as 3 is E.

Remember that the system of music reading and writing has worked for centuries. It is not difficult, and once learned, is yours forever. It is far more difficult to rely on a gimmick and then try to make the transition. Unlike string and wind instruments, where the fingering produces a certain pitch, notes on a piano can technically be played by any finger.

Middle C is generally the first note anyone learns, as it is the note that marks the correct sitting location. Find all the C's on the piano. Then find all the rest of the notes (in any order) in all the ranges. It is very important to get accustomed to the full range of the keyboard. Do this at home (as well as at this lesson), on your own instrument, even if it seems silly. *Listen* carefully to each note, which will begin ear training.

The Grand Staff. This consists of the treble or G clef, and its staff (lines and spaces, for the notes) and the bass or F clef and its staff. The two clefs together cover the entire range of the piano, the treble for the higher range (to the right) and the bass for the lower (to the left), but occasionally, they overlap. The right hand can play in the bass range, and vice versa.

You will need to learn the notes of the grand staff. The well-known mnemonic devices are the only learning aids I recommend (and once chosen, don't change them; this is not a situation that demands "political correctness")

> **Treble clef:**
>> Every good boy does fine (line notes) E G B D F
>> FACE (space notes)
>
> **Bass clef:**
>> Good boys do fine always (line notes) G B D F A
>> All cows eat grass (space notes) A C E G

Notes that don't "fit" onto the staff have ledger lines (Middle C is a good example). You will need to learn a few of these right away, the ones around Middle C, on both clefs.

You won't learn all this overnight. Allow a few weeks. Keep in mind that once learned, there aren't that many more notes to learn, except in the extreme ranges.

The expression "C Position" creates more confusion that it solves. It is really unnecessary verbiage, as the student will be hopefully beyond that range in a couple of weeks. "Five finger" position is more helpful.

Playing the piano is not exactly like touch typewriting, but the less you look directly at the keys, the better your musical reading will be. You will want to find the correct keys without looking, to reinforce the visual note with the physical touch.

Five-finger exercises. Exercises promote finger strength, which in turn develops control, power, balance, flexibility and dexterity. For best results, practice slowly, pressing into the keys. You can do these anytime you have a few minutes to spare. If you separate them from the regular practice time, they might seem less of a chore. Some students find these mind-clearing and relaxing.

RHYTHM.

The absolute basics of music are pitch and rhythm. The correct pitch, or note, is what you learn in note reading.
So you must first find the correct note, and then, know how long to hold it. Traditional music is divided into measures (also called bars). There is a time signature (meter signature) given at the beginning of a piece, next to the clefs, consisting of two numbers. The top number indicates how many beats in a measure. Each measure of the piece will have the same number of beats. The bottom number indicates what type of note gets one beat (4 means a quarter note). For the first lesson, an explanation of whole, half, and quarter notes should be sufficient to learn a short tune. Again, this might sound like a tall order, but once you know that a half note equals two quarters, and so on, this never changes.

SUMMARY OF FIRST LESSON.

Teacher's policies
Sitting correctly at the piano, hand position
Introduction of Middle C and the musical alphabet (find all the C's, etc.)
Grand staff: treble and bass clefs
Basic music notation, pitch and rhythm
Importance of listening

Five finger exercise
A melody or two, with treble and bass clefs, perhaps a famous theme, such as *Ode to Joy*
Method book to purchase:

Unfortunately, Beethoven never wrote the basic method he was planning. Some teachers have a definite preference. Others are willing to use materials that you may already have. There really is no ideal method; most have their good points and some drawbacks. Some survive the test of time, while others become dated.

My suggestion is to get through a basic adult book as quickly as possible (anyone 12 and older can easily use an adult method) and get on to some real piano music, composed for the piano, not arrangements or transcriptions. Younger children will need age-appropriate materials, which may include the use of additional method books. Method books have their defenders, but are not the best way to progress.

Notebook: most teachers will write assignments and comments. Later on, you may also need music manuscript paper.

How long to practice:
At first, ten minutes a day is sufficient. Two five minute sessions per day are even better. You may not get to the piano every day, but make that the regular goal.

To the student, after the first lesson: Please do not be overwhelmed. Your fingers will probably "shoot out" at first, not doing as your teacher described. Remember that your fingers have never done this before, and it will take a few weeks to feel comfortable.

There might seem to be a lot of new things to learn. Bear in mind that the musical alphabet has only seven letters, and these notes, once learned, will never change. They will be yours forever.

`After about six weeks of practice (ten minutes a day, most days) you should be able to look back and see how far you've come, and how the hand position no longer feels odd.

To reap the most benefits from your lessons:
Keep to as regular a schedule as possible, for both daily practice and lessons.

Add a few minutes extra practice in the odd moments of the day, for instance, when you are waiting for someone or something.

Have a notebook for the teacher to write in, and for you to jot down any questions that arise during the week (make a pencil mark on the music, and write down the page number) and bring these questions to your lessons.

A pocket folder is useful if your teacher gives handouts or photocopies. You want to stay organized, and pages quickly multiply and end up lost.

Go to your lesson even if you didn't get much chance to practice. Be honest with the teacher, and many other things can be taught.

You will probably feel that you never play as well at lessons. Your teacher really does understand this. "I played it perfectly at home" is a familiar refrain.

YOUR MUSICAL LIBRARY

Your first pieces (not "songs" as songs are sung) will probably be chosen from your basic method book. Most likely, your teacher will suggest a particular choice if you have to purchase one. There are many such texts available, and there is not one in particular to be recommended absolutely for all students. Every book will have pieces that seem outdated, or that you don't particularly like. It is certainly not necessary to plod through the book, learning each and every piece. You need to grasp the essentials, practice some finger exercises, and move onto "real" piano music as soon as possible. The first volume of any adult method is usually enough material to cover the basic essentials of note reading and rhythm.

Good materials, originally written for piano, which can be incorporated into lessons fairly early on, include some selections found in:
Kabalevsky, Dmitri. *24 Pieces for Children*, op. 39.
Bartók, Béla. *The First Term at the Piano*, and *Mikrokosmos*, Books 1 and 2.

Once you are well on your way to finishing the method book, you should acquire:
Hanon, *The Virtuoso Pianist* (complete). Don't be frightened of the title, and the complete volume is far more economical and useful. There is a *Junior Hanon*, for younger students.
A scale book, which includes all the cadences and arpeggios. A good one is published by Alfred, entitled *The Complete Book of Scales, Chords, Arpeggios & Cadences*, by Willard Palmer, Morton Manus, and Amanda Vick Lethco.

An anthology of keyboard literature (here "keyboard" refers to music written before the invention of the piano) Two good choices include:
Hinson, Maurice, ed. *Essential Keyboard Repertoire*, vols. 1 and 2. (Alfred)
Agay, Denes, ed. *Easy Classics to Moderns* (Music for the Millions series) There are more volumes here also. These volumes contain real music, no transcriptions or arrangements, and are good value.

Your teacher may request a "manuscript" notebook, which has ruled lines for the music staves.

A dictionary of musical terms is very useful to have. *The Essential Dictionary of Music*, by L. C. Harnsberger (Alfred) packs a great deal of information into an economical volume (information on composers and theory as well as definitions of terms)

Where to buy music. If you are near a large, well-stocked music store, you are indeed fortunate. It is so much nicer to be able to look at the music before buying it. Local music stores will most likely order for you, even if they don't normally stock your request (it helps to have the publisher and number, if possible). For those who like to order on line, there is Amazon.com and Sheetmusicplus.com., but I personally feel that it is important to support your local music store.

If your teacher loans you music, ask whether you should purchase your own copy, as too many "loan copies" never find their way back to the teacher's library. The teacher may lend music for brief use, and not think it essential to purchase.

A word about photocopying. While one page or short piece from a collection may be photocopied for educational use, it is so much nicer to have real music, in bound volumes, with the right size and weight of the paper. These form the cornerstones of your music library. It is also important to support the health of the music publishing industry. If your teacher does give you photocopies and handouts, you should find a way to organize them. Perhaps a narrow binder for theory work, and file folders or pocket folders for music. Pages that belong together should be taped. Too many loose pages lead to confusion and loss.

What about CD's? Publishers and proponents of the recording industry will not agree with me, but the use of recordings actually *impedes* learning, by teaching the student to *imitate* what is heard; in essence, it is learning "by ear" instead of learning to figure it out by the notation, which is what learning music is all about. Music is not a foreign language for which you play a CD over and over in order to copy the sound. Learning by ear works for simple tunes, but the student quickly gets lost when things get slightly more complicated (a common point for quitting because of discouragement). There is also the important factor of *time*: all this listening and replaying takes up valuable time that is much better spent practicing.

When I was a university student, a visiting composer denounced recordings as "canned music" in his first lecture. Most of the music students, who were struggling to build a small personal collection of recordings, were taken aback. While it is desirable to build such a library for music appreciation and enjoyment, you should also listen to live broadcasts, attend concerts, and listen to multiple interpretations of the same composition.

There is a world of difference between live and recorded performances (the latter are of course devoid of "mistakes" and can be artificially enhanced in many directions) as there are many nuances and variations of interpretation among the performers and conductors.

THE FIRST SIX MONTHS: MAKING PROGRESS

After about six weeks of lessons, take a look back, and see how much you have already accomplished. Pieces that have been learned. Allow several weeks (longer if your lessons are less frequent than once a week) for the hand position, names of the notes, concepts of rhythm, and the terms you are learning to be absorbed, It may well seem like a tall order to digest all this, and every time you think you have learned everything thus far, new terms are thrown at you. Again, just like note reading, terms like staccato and legato, sharps and flats: once you have learned them, they never change.

Aim to practice ten minutes per day for the first few weeks. Most likely, you won't get to practice every day, but make it a goal anyhow. Think of music as an integral part of your life, a pursuit, rather than a chore. It is better to practice ten minutes a day, rather than skipping a few days and trying to cram all your practice into a half hour. The more repetitions at different times, the better. *Listen* to yourself play, not merely for correct notes, but the kinds of sounds your fingers are making. This is more important than physical technique.

Beginning theory can be introduced almost immediately. Theory explains, enlightens, and enhances one's knowledge of music, as well as making it easier to play. Such study can fill in some time gaps in the weeks when the student feels not enough progress is being made. Theory is the key to understanding music, not just the music you play, but everything you hear. The study of theory can be compared to reading a language as well as speaking it. Knowing what the music is all about makes for a more intelligent, seasoned performance, like driving to a destination you already know versus searching for house numbers or streets, or understanding more about a painting, once details of the background, symbolism, and technique have been pointed out.

It is possible, and not that unusual, for players to reach more advanced levels with no theory or listening skills whatsoever. However enthusiastic they are, they cannot "hear" the sounds they are making, and continue pounding the keys, blurring the pedal, and making stylistic errors. Without theory skills, the reading and interpretation of music will always be much more difficult.

Review what you have learned, in an occasional "review session" of the pieces you have learned, and theory that has been covered. Your understanding of how music "works" will become clearer and start to make sense (remember high school geometry?) Once you know what a chord is, and can hear it, you will always retain this skill. A "C" chord is always a "C" chord. Another benefit of theory is that it facilitates the transition to popular music.

TECHNIQUE. The biggest drawback to advancing in your studies is lack of sufficient technique. By technique, I mean the ability to play with strength, control, dexterity, balance, and accuracy. Remember the old adage that Rome was not built in a day, and that this will take some time to develop.

Theory and music appreciation can fill in the gaps along the way. Set aside a few minutes each day for exercises, perhaps in odd moments or "dead" time and you can accomplish a great deal. Doing exercises away from your regular practice can make them seem less of a chore.

While children find exercises boring, many adults find them relaxing, good as a transfer from the work day. Remember that the thumb and index finger are much stronger than the other three fingers, which need more work to increase their power.

Approximate schedule for technical exercises:

First lesson: five finger pattern on C, to be followed by more such patterns soon.

Within the first month: scale of C, hands separately, up to two octaves. Hands together in contrary motion, two octaves (start with two thumbs on Middle C)
Scales are the means to maneuverability as well as the understanding of key signatures and theory. Usually, they are not introduced soon enough.

Three to six months: five finger patterns on all twelve notes, including a broken and block triad.
Scales of C, G, F, A minor, three octaves, hands separately.
Scale of C, contrary motion, three octaves.

Now the student is ready to begin Hanon, *The Virtuoso Pianist*. As stated previously, do not be intimidated by the title. I have always wondered whether Charles-Louis Hanon (1819-1900), a piano teacher, had any clue that his name would become a household word in the world of piano students. Everyone learns Hanon.

How you practice your exercises is very important and determines whether or not you are wasting time. Now is the time to check your hand position. Press firmly into the keys and listen to the sound of the individual note. Your ears are just as important as your fingers. It is a waste of time to play too fast. You need enough finger pressure to develop strength, and enough slowness for clarity.

TIPS:
Five finger patterns also teach you the basic twelve triads. Again, once you learn what a C chord is, it is always the same.
Scales: once you know the pattern of the C scale, you know the pattern for almost 14 scales (two scales are one hand alike only). Don't learn any new scale without realizing what pattern it follows. Always take note of the sharps and flats in a scale, and try to remember them. Repetition can be boring, so the more variations you have in your exercise repertoire, the better. Suggestions will be given later in this book.
There are hurdles, humps, and plateaus as you move along in lessons. Keep this in mind if you are feeling discouraged at any point.
Practice time should be gradually increased to a half hour. Hopefully practicing will unwittingly become an integral part of your day, and not seem a chore. When you practice even longer, without realizing that time has passed, you are well on your way.

LEARNING A NEW PIECE OF MUSIC: HOW TO APPROACH A PIECE

When a new work of music is put in front of you, you should take a quick survey of it before plunging right in. A great deal of what is to follow is simply common sense, but you want to train yourself to check for these items automatically, as many people will overlook a title that has important meaning as to how the work should sound.

Look for:
Title: is there a descriptive title, or a more generic one?
If it's descriptive, that gives you a good idea. If it's more generic, like "minuet" or "etude" you still have gleaned some information.

Composer (in the upper right corner, unless it is part of a set by the same composer, in which the composer's name will be on the title page) Have you heard of this composer? If not, are dates given? Dates give the clue to the period and style of the composition.

Key Signature and Time Signature. Extremely important, and often overlooked.

Any other directions, including the tempo, which is your least concern at present.

Once you have completed this overview, proceed to the actual music, and **the big three** here are
Correct pitch (correct notes)
Correct rhythm
Workable fingering

Correct pitch. Don't be concerned about "mistakes" as the important point is to be able to hear when a note is the wrong one. You want to train your ear to hear the correct pitch, then for the various subtleties of the tone.

Correct rhythm. *Rhythmic mistakes are the most difficult to correct*; it seems that you must unlearn before you can relearn. So it is advisable to spend some extra time originally, working out exactly where all the beats are. Observe all rests carefully. More will be said about that later.

Workable fingering. Many fingering options are actually possible, as everyone's hands are different. Always observe any fingering suggestions that are offered. If anything seems unusual, try to figure out why (sometimes you have to look at the whole phrase, and work backwards). Once a fingering pattern is decided, keep it *consistent*, no changing. It should be logical, employing the fingers in order, as much as possible, following the learned patterns (scales, arpeggios).

REFINEMENTS: to "polish" a piece, and have it sound as the composer intended, certain refinements are necessary: dynamics, articulation, phrasing, and style of the period.

Dynamics describe the volume: loud, soft, and all degrees in between. Consider the time that the piece was written, and how loud a *forte* might actually have been.

Articulation refers to how you "attack" a note: staccato, legato, lightly detached, and here also are many degrees of difference. Staccato is not simply a "hot potato" as there are many degrees of staccato. Pedaling, if appropriate, could be listed here.

Phrasing is usually described as performing musical "sentences" and the expression put therein. The way a performer shapes the phrase determines how a piece sounds. Consider listening to a speaker delivering in a monotone. Music needs the same sorts of improvements in order to come alive. Where is the high point of the phrase? Try breathing as if you were putting words to the music.

Correct style of the period. As you learn more about the eras of musical history, you will begin to develop a sense of style; for instance, you would not play Bach the same way that you play Chopin.

Tempo. *Always the last item on the list.* Never practice a piece too fast, especially in the early stages of learning. You want your fingers to learn the notes ("muscle memory") and if you play too fast, this will not happen. The choice of tempo can vary, as you should find the comfortable range where the piece "works" (too slow can be deadly, but if too fast, you are literally throwing it away, as the notes disappear before they can be assimilated).

Marking your music. Some teachers mark a student's music excessively, even including the date. The music then becomes extremely cluttered and difficult to read. Other teachers are at the other extreme, and feel that the music should remain pristine. Certain markings I find useful. Circling essential fingerings can be very helpful (by essential, I mean the finger that determines the whole passage). Circle notes, sharps, rests, other directions (e.g., ritardando, abbreviated to rit.) only after you find yourself making the same mistake repeatedly.

PROGRESS REPORT.
It is impossible to give exact time frames for learning music, as so much depends on how much time the student has to practice, and whether the practice is efficient.
Once you are playing the pieces from the anthologies of piano literature, you can look back and see how far you have come. You are now ready for more of the music of the composers you have been studying, including selected works from

Bach, J. S. *Notebook for Anna Magdalena Bach*
Bartók, Béla. *For Children*
Kabalevsky, Dmitri. *Children's Pieces*, op. 27
Schumann, Robert. *Album for the Young*, op. 68.

Older students should not be put off by the titles; adults play these pieces far better than children do.

If there is a piece (anything at all: a popular song, something seasonal) that you really want to learn, don't be afraid to ask your teacher. Anything that is not originally written for piano is an arrangement, and something suitable can be found. For the classical pieces you might aspire to, it is better to wait awhile before tackling The "Moonlight" Sonata, but you could attempt easier pieces by Beethoven, and learn more about the style and interpretation. Any "watered down" arrangements of real piano pieces are not recommended.

ADULT RESTARTERS

I must have been about twelve years old when some new friends of my parents were visiting, and the woman observed the music I was working on, Mozart's *Fantasia in D minor*. She said that she used to play that, but couldn't play anymore because her fingers would not "move" to the notes. Children didn't comment aloud then, but I remember being privately distressed, that someone who had spent so much time learning the piano presumably could no longer play. What I did not know then was that she could have easily regained her skills.

If you had piano lessons in your youth, you can regain your skills steadily, and play better than ever. For a smoother review, it is a good idea to start at a slightly easier level that the most difficult pieces you played in the past.

Many compositions are written technically so young learners can play them, but they are much better performed by adults, including the previously mentioned works, and sets of pieces like Schumann's *Kinderszenen*, op. 15, and Debussy's *Children's Corner*.

Getting back in shape, and reviewing what you already have learned: start working on the Hanon exercises the scales you have had. These will build strength. You might be ready for exercises by Pischna, or some of the *51 Exercises* by Johannes Brahms (here again, do not be intimidated, as your teacher will pick out the most immediately useful). Try doing some of this work in the odd moments of the day. Making good use of such time is excellent reinforcement for learning, and will make practice seem like less of a chore. This same routine will prove useful if you have been traveling, and did not get to practice for awhile.

You may have a special piece in mind that you wish to learn. Ask your teacher's advice. Sometimes, a more difficult composition can be learned surprisingly well when the student is highly motivated. If the choice is far too difficult at the present, perhaps another piece by the same composer can be substituted.

A solid foundation: in addition to the technical studies mentioned above, for a "balanced diet" musically, you need to learn works from the various periods of music history:
Baroque (ca 1600-1750)
Classic (ca 1750-1820)
Note that classic refers to the style of the period, not "classic" as opposed to "popular"
Romantic (19th century)
Impressionistic (late 19th and early 20th centuries)
20th century music

In the interest of efficient practice, a large work, such as a sonata, should be balanced with shorter pieces. You want to learn the literature without being overwhelmed. Three to four works at one time are usually sufficient. Some students find that they want only one or two. Detailed lists are included in this book.

When you are learning the piano music of the various composers, this study can be a springboard to music appreciation and history. It is extremely useful to listen to chamber music and orchestral works by the same composers you are currently studying: you want to hear their style, harmonies, dynamics, rhythmic patterns. The piano music will begin to make more sense.

This would be a good time to acquire a music dictionary if you don't already have one, plus a guide to "classical" music which gives information on the composers and stylistic eras, hopefully with illustrations. The usage of the term "classical" is explained above. If the book gives listening recommendations, bear in mind that these are one person's opinion, and another book might recommend something different. Once you find out that Brahms wrote four symphonies, you will want to hear them all eventually, and many times more than once.

THEORY: after reviewing scales, it would be a good time to learn how the Circle of Fifths is designed and works, and start learning the key signatures, intervals, and basic triads. Learning is far more thorough if you write in your music manuscript notebook. If you like flash cards, you can make some or purchase them, and study them in odd moments. Practice the cadences that are given with each scale in the scale book. Pay attention to the interval of a fifth, which is the key to a great deal of understanding the musical system.

I have seen some students' strange methods of ascertaining what a key signature means, without any understanding or feeling of being in that key whatsoever. Sharps and flats follow definite patterns; they are not simply hanging in space, awaiting identification.

"I have repeatedly had students come for instruction who have after great effort prepared one, two, or at the most three show pieces, even pieces as far advanced s the Tchaikovsky or the Liszt Concerto, who barely knew what key they were playing in." Josef Lhevinne, *Basic Principles in Pianoforte Playing*.

By sensing what key you are in, you will read and play more musically, through better navigation, knowing what chords are leading where. The Circle of Fifths will direct you, and your playing will make more sense. This whole approach is an introduction to harmony, which can be among the most rewarding of studies. Harmony is to music what color is to art.

RHYTHM: How to improve your sense of it

For those of us who were not born with a natural sense of rhythm, this aspect of music performance is perhaps the most daunting and difficult to master. Pianists have the additional handicap of playing alone, not with a group or orchestra with a leader, and therefore lose out on the benefits of group practice. Their instrumentalist counterparts seem to be miles ahead. Although rhythm is considered the "backbone" of music, and an absolute essential to "get" right, it can be done, and without too much difficulty, if you follow the suggestions.

What is absolutely essential here, which is unfortunately so seldom emphasized, is the sense of *feeling the beat.* You need to sense this pulse *physically*. For those who like imagery, picture an invisible drummer in the background, or a conductor keeping the beat for you.

Many teachers count (and write) out the patterns with systems like 1+ -- such as One A and E [I always wondered who "Andy" was] but fail to emphasize the need for feeling *where the actual beats fall*. You need to sense this pulse, or ticking, even if there is a rest, or notes that are held through. *The beat is always there.*

Rhythmic mistakes are the most difficult to correct, as it seems that you have to "unlearn" before you can relearn. Don't try to play a new piece the way you think you heard it; learn to work out the rhythmic patterns on your own (working backwards through the measure if necessary).

Find a method of counting that you can live with. Counting aloud, the least liked, is actually the least beneficial, as you are listening to your own voice rather than your playing, and may not have the beats pulsing correctly. You might tap your foot, or tap your toe inside your shoe, or beat one hand while practicing with the other. I like the foot tapping technique, but this is for learning and practice. For actual performance, it would be more advisable to use the tapping the toe inside the shoe, for aesthetic reasons.

For measures that seem complicated:
Pencil in the actual beats (1, 2, 3, 4, for example) with small vertical lines (not numbers). You simply have to figure out where the beats actually fall. This method, incidentally, leads to better phrasing, and avoidance of the so-called "tyranny of the bar line".

You might try adding a heavy accent to the first beat of the bar. This is totally unmusical, but it will help you find the structure initially. If you know you are adding the ascent deliberately, you can easily lighten it up later on.

Double the time. By this I mean counting in eighth notes rather than quarters. This will prove invaluable in many situations.

Metronomes (M.M. means Maelzel's Metronome). The good news here is, you don't have to have one. The student may breathe a sigh of relief. Teachers (and music majors) should have one, for demonstration, to check suggested tempi, and determine erratically played sections, for instance, rushing, or other imbalances. The metronome is not the panacea for rhythm, as it is a machine, and, as no one wants to play robotically, it is impossible to practice with.

Rests. No discussion of rhythm could be complete without discussing rests, as they are *just as important as the actual notes*. They form an integral and essential part of what a composer is trying to say. Bear in mind that up until around 1830, composers had to use quill pens. It would have been much easier to write whole or half notes; if there is a rest, they really do mean it! Observing the rests is part of the means of making a work of music come alive: the rests give buoyancy, tension,, and propel the work. This idea has been taken to another level in the twentieth century, focusing on silence.

A common pianistic pitfall is to keep your fingers lingering on a note or notes that should have been released. This is all too easy to do, especially if you don't notice any dissonant or clashing sounds, and there is a nice harmonic pattern. A wind or string player has to get off the note in order to reach the next one, breathe or change bowing, but the pianist can simply let the notes sit.

"The notes I handle no better than many pianists. But the pauses between the notes- ah, that is where the art resides." Artur Schnabel quoted in the *Chicago Daily News*, 1958.

BASIC TRAINING: BACH

The importance of learning the music of Johann Sebastian Bach cannot be overemphasized; it could easily be argued that Bach is to music what Shakespeare is to English. "Bach is good for the soul as well as for the body, and I recommend that you never lose touch with him." Josef Hofmann, *Piano Playing, with piano questions answered.*

Everyone should study Bach. All the composers who followed him did. By studying Bach, you receive a true *music* lesson: how to follow a theme without getting lost, how to balance musical lines (these are usually called "voices" although no one is singing), independence of the two hands, plus finger strength and dexterity. Yes, often his music seems complicated, but the study of it will repay you more than a thousandfold. Many famous musicians begin their day with practicing Bach. If you are an early riser, this is a lovely time of day to experience Bach's music.

Ask someone who hasn't studied music what their favorite classical piece is, and the answer is usually Ravel's *Bolero*, or sometimes Pachelbel's *Canon*. Why these? Because the themes are repeated over and over, and the listener gets a chance to grasp what is going on musically. Most orchestral works of any length (symphonies, for example) simply sound too dense or overly complex to the untrained ear, as there is too much going on at once (*too many notes*: you may remember that line from *Amadeus*) as opposed to a more melodically oriented composer like Tchaikovsky.

Once you train your ear by the study of Bach, this skill will enable you to navigate through the major musical literature. The works will start to make sense.

After learning some of the shorter pieces in the Notebook for Anna Magdalena Bach (his second wife) you are ready to begin some of the Short Preludes. Opinions have been voiced that these little treasures are not nearly studied enough, and I agree.

Sometimes this collection of preludes is termed Little Preludes, and the order of the pieces varies in different editions. Your teacher will help you decide where to begin (the preludes are not in order of difficulty). A good one to begin with is the C major, BWV 939, followed by the F major BWV 927.

You will see numbers with the preludes, either B.W.V. numbers or S. numbers. B.W.V. stands for Bach Werke Verzeichnis (catalog of Bach's works) which was compiled by Wolfgang Schmieder (hence the S. number). Bach did not assign opus numbers to his works. This catalog places the works by categories: cantatas, instrumental music, etc. rather than the usual chronological format used for later composers.

An interesting footnote to Bach studies is the fact that he is the only composer whose works are widely adaptable, in arrangements such as those by the Empire Brass, and have been successfully transformed into the jazz idiom (The Swingle Singers, the Jacques Loussier Trio). Listen to the recordings of the late (and now legendary) Glenn Gould, some of which were chosen to be put on a spacecraft.

By the time you are learning the short preludes of Bach, you are now ready to begin some of the literature listed in this book. Try for the balanced musical diet, including something from each period in turn, balancing longer works with shorter ones. Try to learn at least two or three pieces by each composer. If you don't particularly like one piece, try another. The piece that is not to your liking may not even be typical of that composer. It is important to learn enough about each composer (and listen to other works as well) to get a feel for the composer's personal style. When you study a composer long enough, you will begin to recognize the composer's personal trademarks, the hallmarks of a style no other composer has.

You are on a voyage of discovery; keep listening to music, taking note of any works you particularly enjoy. The composer probably has written piano music that you can explore. Practically every great composer (and conductor also) with few exceptions, was a pianist first.

OPUS NUMBERS and all those other letters. You have already made the acquaintance of Schmieder and the BWV for the works of Bach. Most composers before Beethoven did not use opus numbers. Opus, a Latin word, translates as "work". The opus number is the means of identifying the work. It could be a one page piano piece or an entire opera. If the opus is a set of pieces, the main number will be the opus number, and the other number is the number of the piece in the set, for instance, Chopin's *Preludes*, op. 28, consists of 24 preludes, so the seventh one of the set is Op. 28, no. 7.

For composers whose works are cataloged by a scholar, the scholar's name is given to the number, rather than the word opus. Catalogs are continually being revised, with new scholarship leads to new editions, and in some cases, even new numbers. Generally speaking, the cataloging is chronological, rather than by category, though you will find such divisions in some references.

Some of the more common catalog numbers are, with the composer's name first Scarlatti: Longo or Kirkpatrick (L or K) Haydn: Hoboken (H); Mozart: Köchel (K, or KV, Köchel Verzeichnis); Schubert: Deutsch (D) Beethoven, Schumann, Chopin, Brahms, to name a few, used their own opus numbers. Twentieth century composers have learned from history: usually their music is well annotated.

Scholars are constantly revising, and in rare cases, discovering new works. Where to put the numbers? In an *Anhang* (supplement) sometimes with a letter appended, and if dates and numbers cannot be determined, WoO (*Werke ohne Opus*) a work without an opus number. If sufficient evidence materializes, works are actually renumbered (as in the case of Dvorak's symphonies).

If you decide to compose a small piece right now, you could call it your Opus 1. Write the date on it also.

"APPROACHING A NEW PIECE OF MUSIC"

Some of this is review, with more hints and ideas for learning to follow. Try to make observing these essentials an automatic habit:
Title of the work
Composer
Key signature (what scale is this piece using? Check Circle of Fifths, look at how the piece ends: what chord is it?)
Time signature
Tempo marking (merely observe for now)
Any other directions or instructions

You can already glean a great deal from the above, even before striking a single key. Does the title give you any information? Who is the composer? If unknown, are any dates given? Is the piece an original composition for piano, or is it an arrangement, accompaniment, transcription? You should have a basic idea of the style (Baroque, Romantic, etc.) and what sort of mood the composer is trying to convey (rain, moonlight, e.g., if it is a descriptive piece) a classical sonata, a dance form, something influenced by folk music.

Observe the length of the work, and look for any sections with repeat marks. Check over the first few pages, searching for any patterns or sections that recur. Try sight reading the piece through. Whether or not to try hands together immediately is a personal decision. Some pieces simply "go together" much more easily than others where the hands have to be worked out separately. If any rhythmic patterns seem daunting, stop, and figure them out, remembering that rhythmic mistakes are the most difficult to correct.

After a first run-through, you are now in a position to see which measures will need extra work. Stop and work out the fingerings. Always look at any suggested fingering, but don't be afraid to change it if you find something better for your hand.

The important point is, keep the fingering constant (don't change it each time you play). Everyone's hands are different, and the same fingering patterns are not a one-size-fits-all, though there are many passages that can really be fingered one way.

Watch for any accidentals, and remember that the accidental, whether a sharp, flat, or natural, "powers" all the notes of that pitch within the bar. Think of an accidental as a "red flag" if you often miss repeated pitches.

Always **listen** to the sound of the piece, and the sounds you are making when playing it. Igor Stravinsky was asked about Schoenberg's article, *Heart and Brain in Music*. Which of the two (heart or brain) is more important? "Neither, my dear," he countered with a broad smile. "The ear," he corrected. (Quoted by Glenn Watkins in *The Gesualdo Hex*)

Mark anything you don't understand, in order to ask your teacher at the next lesson.

SIGHT READING should be mentioned here, as the better you become at sight reading, the easier new music will be to learn, plus you can cover a great deal of musical literature much faster, and sort out the pieces you wish to work on more thoroughly. You will also be able to accompany others (vocalists, instrumentalists, choruses) with greater ease and confidence.

Excellent materials for sight reading include folk songs, community song books, hymns, Christmas carols, popular songs. That old box of music from someone's attic might yield some treasures (check out used book sales as well). Take note that if the music is really "vocal" music, like a hymn or carol, the parts will be written for soprano, alto, tenor, bass so the stems of the notes will not be written as for piano music, and the eighth and sixteenth notes are not joined with the "beam" or bar, as they are in instrumental music; they are written with "flags". This is not at all difficult to get used to, once you are aware of the difference.

Now to get to the actual practice: For pieces that seem more difficult, work in "doable" sections, don't bite off more than you can chew. Isolate the tough measures, and analyze what the problem is: fingering, note reading, rhythm. Bear in mind that some pieces may "look easy" but in fact are quite tricky once you get into them, and vice versa: there are many works that look hard to read, and don't sight read easily at all, but once you have figured out the notes, it's smooth sailing. For the truly tough spots, make certain that you have correct fingering both entering and leaving the passage, and do not change the fingering. Working on a measure in isolation can otherwise be more than useless.

Difficult sections need to be drilled on their own, several repetitions at a time. The folk wisdom of my student days used to be "play it correctly three times in a row, without hesitation, and it's yours". I don't know if this is true, but it is a close to truth if all other guidelines are followed.

Once a piece is "getting off the ground", take a scrutinizing look for any missed details: staccato, legato, rests, dynamics, changes in tempo. If the piece calls for the use of the pedal, you should add it now, if you haven't before. The pedal should be an integral part of the piece, not put on later like the frosting on a cake.

Phrasing and Interpretation.
These terms signify what makes a piece come alive, conveying what the composer intended to say. What exactly is a musical phrase? We speak of musical "sentences" conveying musical "thoughts". Breathe. Much can be gleaned about phrasing from the standpoint of a singer or wind player: where would you have to take a breath? Or change a bow, if you are a string player? Where are the notes going, in other words, is there a high point? Where does the music seem to be getting louder or softer? Is there a fading away, or a slam-bang ending?

Some ideas are best grasped in the negative, however unfortunate that may sound. Much as you would find someone speaking in a monotone quite deadly, the same is true for making music. Phrasing or musical "expression" is what gives a piece life. Here you have the chance for some degree of personal expression, or artistic license, putting in some of your own sense of the style into what the composer is trying to convey (a crisper staccato? Slightly slower tempo?). Do remember that unless you are improvising, such as in a jazz performance, you as a performer are duty bound to try to relay exactly what the composer wrote, in the correct style of the period, which still leaves leeway (compare recordings of the same composition and you will find differences of artistic opinion.)

Tempo. The last consideration, as the slightest increase in speed can make a total muddle of all your careful work. Try your piece at various speeds. Check out any metronome indications. A tempo has to "fit" like a good pair of shoes. Too fast, and not only could it fall apart, but also might be indiscernible to the listener's ear. Too slow, and it could be deadly. Look at the fastest sections of the piece, and judge from those. I have heard works of Bach played at such high speed that they are almost unrecognizable, not understandable to anyone unfamiliar with the work. Virtuosity is not the goal, what the composer is trying to say, is.

THE PEDALS

Much mystique surrounds the technique of pedaling, thereby perpetuating this aura. Volumes have been written about various aspects of pedaling. Some teachers even forbid the use of the pedal before a certain number of years of study.

The most important part of the body regarding the pedal is not the foot, but the **ear**. Now, more than ever, you must listen more keenly to the sounds you are producing, as the pedal not only enhances the sound, it can blur it into cacophony.

There are three pedals, although some pianos will only have two. By far, the most commonly used pedal is the **Damper Pedal (*tre corde*)** which is the one on the right. This pedal is also sometimes called the "loud" pedal, or the sustaining pedal, but the middle pedal (the one omitted on some instruments) is also sometimes called the sustaining pedal). The damper pedal raises the dampers (look inside your piano as your foot depresses the pedal) so everything connects and blends.

Listening must be done very accurately, in order to time the release of the pedal correctly. The technique is not difficult to grasp, once you actually begin doing it.

General guidelines: Sometimes markings are given in the music, below the grand staff, usually put in by editors, but do take note of them. Change the pedal when the harmony changes. The pedal is for tonal enhancement, not as a substitute for legato (your fingers should do any "connecting" and using the pedal to do this is not advisable). Do not use this pedal in Bach, almost never in Haydn and Mozart, sparingly in Beethoven.

For the 19th century and later composers (Chopin, Schumann, Mendelssohn, Brahms, Debussy, Ravel) the pedal is essential, and the composers assume you will use it. Some 20th century composers have precisely written instructions for the pedal, probably because they have observed improper use. Some people get so enthusiastic with the pedal they treat it like the gas pedal of an automobile, and forget to listen.

The pedal will take some getting used to, as pedals vary in resistance from piano to piano. It's best merely to start getting the feel of the pedals, literally. Make sure you have shoes that enable you to feel what your foot is doing. The thinner the shoe, the better, even slippers or socks. Sneakers, heavier shoes, and boots are counterproductive.

Una corda **("soft") pedal).** This pedal is the one on the left. It cuts the volume of sound by shifting the keyboard slightly to the right, so the hammers strike two instead of three strings (or one string where there are two). The quality of the sound is also changed. You want to be able to use this pedal when needed, but you don't want it to become a crutch. You need to expand your range of dynamics to be able to play softly (but clearly) with your fingers, and the pedal supplies the extra level.

Middle ("sustaining" or *sostenuto*) pedal. This one is not found on all pianos, and will be the one you do not have, if your piano has only two pedals. This permits the sustaining of notes, without blurring, such as a low bass note while the hands are needed elsewhere (high in the treble range, for example). You will seldom use this, but it is extremely useful in certain instances.

TIPS FOR GOOD PRACTICE HABITS

KEEP LISTENING!

In order to get the most value for practice time, remember that several shorter sessions are far better than one longer one.

Don't keep returning to the beginning of the piece every time you make a mistake (everyone does this) as the beginning keeps getting better, and the more difficult spots aren't being addressed.

For any difficult spots where the problem is fingering, make sure you have the flow of the fingering coming from the previous measures [the "lead-in"] and moving onto the next ones. You could find an "ideal" fingering for the measure by itself, and it might not work when reinserted in the piece.

Isolate any hard spots, and practice these separately, perhaps in odd moments of the day (the same advice as for exercises)

Try beginning your practice with a different order of pieces every day. A few warm-up exercises are fine, but do not spend too much time on them, or you will feel tired before you have gotten to the toughest work.

If you are having serious trouble with a piece, several times in a row, practice something else, or go do something else, before returning to the original piece. This seems to be a "block" and the brain needs to "reboot". Not in the mood for your assigned lesson: Try sight reading, finding something new, even reviewing.

Marking music: don't mark a whole lot of things into a brand-new piece. Wait to find any difficult spots, where beats should be penciled in, or fingering marked (or circled, if already there). Sometimes *one finger* is a passage is "essential" to the flow; you might want to circle that, and add in a few of your own finger numbers if helpful.

Aim to practice every day. This is most probably not possible, but make it a goal anyway. Try to have a review session occasionally, of works previously learned. Keep a repertoire list at the back of a notebook (if you have pieces in an anthology, you can merely check them off in the table of contents). This will provide a record of what you have learned.

Sight reading is extremely important, and has its own section later.

Ditto for scales, chords, cadences, arpeggios (broken chords). As your knowledge and proficiency increase with scales, chords, technique, sight reading, theory , everything begins to "come together", make sense, and yes, will seem much easier. You will see the "forest", have the "aha" moment, the "big picture", and find that there is a great deal of music you will be able to play without practicing it.

FINE TUNING YOUR PLAYING

The following suggestions are not meant to be nit picking, but refining and polishing, thus making your playing more musical.

Once you have mastered the notes and rhythm, with a workable fingering, you are ready to add the refinements of phrasing, if you haven't incorporated some already.

Articulation and dynamics help the performer make the music "speak" and convey what the composer is trying to say.
Staccato: there are varying degrees of staccato, from very sharp and percussive, to a mezzo staccato where the notes are merely lightly detached
Accents: the same remarks apply
Tenuto markings indicate that the note should be held for its full value
Legato marking can be very short, simple nuances, or long phrase indications

Dynamic markings cover the entire range, with many degrees in between, such as the incremental levels in crescendo and diminuendo (or decrescendo)

The above additions are up to the player's discretion, but the teacher's advice and stylistic considerations should be paramount. The length of the piece, how many sections, are also important, in that you don't want too many little surges, too much emotion, or too extreme a range within a short composition.

Pedaling is definitely a "given" for Romantic period and later compositions, unless indicated otherwise. Pedaling would not work in a brittle toccata, for instance.

The "holding penalty": make sure you are not holding notes that should not be held, especially common with arpeggio passages, or repeated broken chords, such as the Alberti bass. Likewise, make sure you are holding notes through that should be. Train yourself to look for such passages, as you won't hear any clashing notes to indicate a mistake.

Tempo is the last consideration, once you feel comfortable with the notes. A good tempo is like a well fitting pair of shoes, an analogy previously made, but it bears repeating. Too slow can be deadly, too fast, and the piece falls apart. Sometimes you have to look at the whole work (especially in several movements, or separate pieces) to judge how fast a certain movement or piece should be. In general, look at the fastest-moving notes in the piece, and decide how this passage should be played for maximum effect, and you may be surprised how it changes the opening section. Be careful about rushing, or speeding up where it is not desirable. When a piece is loud, people tend to play faster, and vice versa. So you could actually slow down a bit in a fast passage.

Every time you play, always look for **something new**, something you hadn't noticed before. Keep **listening** to your playing, listen for balance, beauty of tone. Are you bringing out the melody, or the most important notes? Often these notes require effort from the weakest fingers, and appear as the top note. Don't "over" emote, pound the keys, or misuse the pedal. Think "through" a few bars of the piece in your mind before you begin.

You want to develop a sense of style, to play your music in the manner of the time when it was written (albeit, on a modern instrument, but following the stylistic guidelines). This entails some knowledge of music history, and goes hand in hand with music appreciation. A balanced musical diet has works from all the main periods. It helps a great deal to get to know some of the composers' other works: orchestral, chamber, vocal. As you become familiar with the kinds of sounds a composer writes, these will transfer to the piano, and enhance your enjoyment and appreciation of concerts and general listening to music.

MEMORIZATION

I have heard many tales of the bad memories associated with June recitals. Many may disagree, but I feel memorization is not necessary for the average player, someone not aspiring to conservatory training or public performance. Memory training, in general, is beyond the scope of this book. A few suggestions are given for those who anticipate fulfilling a requirement or having to teach those who must do so. Concert pianists are expected to perform from memory, a tradition begun in the nineteenth century by Clara Schumann and Franz Liszt. Most other instrumentalists (other than touring soloists) use their music. Chamber music groups and orchestras perform with music. Sometimes you will observe a conductor who is not using a score, but conducting from memory. There are a few pianists who go against the trend and read from their music.

For average players, the better the memorization skill, the poorer the sight reading, and more difficulty reading new music.

The more you memorize, the easier it gets (remember memorizing poems in school?)

What type of memorizer are you? For example,
Does memory come easily, almost automatically?
Do you look at the piano keys for cues?
Do you visualize the music, even to the exact paging, and the markings on it?
Do you "hear" the music in your mind?

Determine what works best for you, and stick with that method.
Don't try to play half from memory, half from music (or have the music on the piano as a safety measure)
Studying the music while away from the keyboard may help
Practicing the piece with the hands an extra octave apart, or in different ranges, one hand much louder, are techniques that have helped some students

Before you begin to play, think through a few bars of the work in your mind (this should be done by players using music also). Testing the waters, so to speak.

SIGHT READING

I put sight reading at the top of the list for advantageous musical skills. It is the means to exploring, getting acquainted with, and learning a large volume of music. Sight reading is the first approach to learning a new work.

The more you can grasp in one fell swoop, the better. It might seem like a tall order: notes, rhythm, phrasing, dynamics, playing with some degree of accuracy, style, and workable fingering. Don't forget to look at the title and for the composer, if given. The more you sight read, the better you will be at it, and you will make the happy discovery that there are pieces you will be able to play without practicing them, Try to do some sight reading at least once a week.
Materials have been suggested previously, and advice given regarding vocal music.

Everyone should know how to play *Happy Birthday* and *The Star Spangled Banner*. You may find some more useful pieces while you are searching through the collections.

PLAYABILITY.

Bear in mind that some pieces simply do not "sight read" well, and are not "sight reader friendly" in today's parlance. There might be some seemingly complicated-looking pattern, wide ranges, a tricky rhythm. Do not immediately write off such a piece as too difficult to learn. Often, sitting quietly with it for a few minutes, figuring out the problem will reveal a solution. Slow down to look at the one measure or one measure at a time. For rhythms especially, it is worth the extra time spent figuring it out slowly and accurately, rather than ingraining a mistake which will be difficult to correct later on.

N.B. This method works for any so-called **problem spot** in a composition. Slow down, isolate it, and work it out. What exactly is the problem: rhythm, fingering, note reading? Five minutes well spent will reward you later. Here you might want to pencil in vertical lines for where the beats lie, or write in some fingering. Make sure you have checked the lead-in to make sure the fingering works. Then don't change it.

POPULAR MUSIC AND JAZZ

If you are a "classical" pianist at heart, who would like to learn some popular music, here are a few suggestions to get you started.

Keep studying theory: learn how the chords work. The principles are the same for all keys, so you do not have to memorize that B-flat 7 goes to E flat, you simply learn that the V7 chord moves to the tonic (I). Most popular music has the chord symbols above the staff, so be sure to observe these.

A beginning jazz method (Alfred has an excellent one) will help you hone your rhythmic skills and sense of the beat. The aforementioned "invisible drummer" should become a major force, and help you to keep a steady beat while you adjust the melody rhythmically, to "jazz it up", so you won't sound like a classical pianist trying to play pop music.

Improvisation involves composing, changing, and altering a melody, a direct opposite of a "classical" piece, where you are morally and musically duty bound to perform what the composer has written. In pop music, you are free to make your own arrangement.

Popular songs are available in sheet music and collections. These are arrangements, so feel free to experiment with what the arranger has done. You might want to add some arpeggiated lines, for starters. Try the main theme in another register, for an echo effect. Later on, you might want to add or change some of the chords. Use your ear!

A collection of oldies from a time period you like, or selections from a favorite musical would be a good idea for material to work on. Play through the song "straight", meaning without alteration, and listen for bare spots or for where alterations might be effective. You have to feel where the beats fall, and what the tune actually is, before making adjustments.

Play "behind" the beat, meaning keep the beat steady in your mind (or your accompaniment) so the melody line can be adjusted. Consider how a pop singer would interpret the lines.

If there is a particular popular or jazz artist you like, find out if the person published a collection of arrangements. You can glean ideas from these. Sometimes the music is quite daunting, much like recipes from celebrated chefs, but don't be discouraged. Many of the outstanding jazz pianists (Oscar Peterson, Art Tatum, Andre Previn, for example) all began as classical pianists.

The ultimate goal would be to be able to play directly from a "fake book" which has the tune and the chord symbols only, no arrangements or accompaniments. But this skill is hardly necessary to have many happy hours enjoying popular music from arrangements. You can always make these your "own" and make them slightly different each time you play.

INTRODUCTION TO PIANO LITERATURE

Keyboard literature is an amazingly vast treasure trove. Before getting into selected works, some pointers for style should be considered, based on the instruments of the time for which the music was composed (hence "keyboard" vs. piano). The earliest pianos had a much weaker sound compared with the grand pianos of today. Just because the piano didn't exist at the time a piece was written doesn't prevent you from playing it on the piano. The composer's style should be taken into account. Any other works that you already have heard by the composer should aid in the quest to learn "what the composer is trying to say" as the printed notes cannot convey everything. Here is a quick checklist, by historical era:

BAROQUE ERA (ca 1600-1750)
No pedal
Strict rhythm, but flowing, no ritards
Balance of the "voices" [individual lines] in contrapuntal music
Attention to entrances of the theme or motif, with clarity and definition
"terraced" dynamics rather than crescendo and decrescendo
Nuances or articulation and accent bring the music to life

CLASSICAL ERA (ca 1750-1820)
No pedal, except in rare instances, for improvement of the sound only, not for legato
Strict rhythm, no ritards, unless specifically indicated, and especially avoid ritards at endings of sections
Clarity of themes (keep them singing) and know where you are navigating, in development and recapitulation sections regarding the themes
"Hear" all the rests, especially at the end of a movement
Dynamics should be at a quieter level, in keeping with the instruments of the time
Keep your playing buoyant: do not keep the notes sounding when they shouldn't be in an Alberti bass or arpeggiated writing
Make the distinction between melody and accompaniment
Polish the ends of phrases (a tiny diminuendo) but keep in strict tempo

ROMANTIC ERA (ca 1820-1900)

Descriptive titles for pieces are often given

More emotion, more leeway with tempi and interpretation of rhythm (use of rubato occurs more often here, though it was not unknown in earlier times)

Pedal is used (composers assume this) but keep listening for clarity

Much greater range of dynamics

A singing theme above an accompaniment occurs often: bring out the top note

Greater range of harmonic progression, in many cases with big chords: the top melody note must be brought out

IMPRESSIONISM (ca 1890-1920)

Makes even more use of the pedal and the harmonic possibilities of pianistic sounds

TWENTIETH CENTURY

Now in most cases, you will have the composer's original indications and markings

Many new harmonies, even key signatures, and means of articulation

For unusual techniques or note reading, directions are usually included

For those interested in art, it is interesting to make comparisons of the stylistic characteristics of the different eras.

KEYBOARD LITERATURE

Composers are listed chronologically by musical period, with selected piano works, not complete listings. The most important names in the canon of piano music are listed in large type

RENAISSANCE
Note: dance forms were among the earliest forms of instrumental pieces. In this period, the pavane and gaillarde were often composed
English virginalists of the Elizabethan era:
William Byrd (1543-1623)
John Bull (c1562-1628)
Orlando Gibbons (1583-1625)
The most important collections of their works are *Parthenia* and *The Fitzwilliam Virginal Book*

BAROQUE
Note: many works by these composers are entitled <u>suites</u>. These are sets of pieces in dance forms, the four obligatory ones being the allemande, courante, sarabande, and gigue, with other pieces in dance forms added. French composers gave descriptive titles to the pieces within the suites (a tradition followed by later French composers) Preludes and fugues were other important forms in this period, with Bach's *Well-Tempered Clavier* as forming the canon of piano music, along with Beethoven's sonatas

Henry Purcell (1659-1695) *Suites*
Francois Couperin (1668-1733) *Pieces de clavecin*
    also wrote *The Art of Playing the Harpsichord*
Jean-Philippe Rameau (1683-1764) *Pieces de clavecin*
    also wrote a *Treatise on Harmony*

JOHANN SEBASTIAN BACH (1685-1750) *The Well-Tempered Clavier* (2v) *Two and Three Part Inventions*, French and *English Suites*, *Partitas, Italian Concerto, Goldberg Variations*, several concertos for clavier

Georg Frideric Handel (1685-1759) *Suites*

Domenico Scarlatti (1685-1757) over 550 *Sonatas* (these are in binary form, and originally were entitled *Esercizi*)

CLASSIC PERIOD

It is important to know that the "sonata-allegro" form, also called classical sonata form, derives from this period. Stemming from the binary forms of the Baroque, such as the sonatas of Scarlatti, it was developed by Haydn and then further by Mozart and Beethoven. To play compositions in this form effectively, you need to know how to navigate the themes and development. In addition, Haydn is named the father of the symphony and string quartet, and Mozart is credited with the development of the piano concerto. Beethoven's piano sonatas form the cornerstone of piano literature.

C.P.E. Bach (1714-1788) *Sonatas*, and the well-known student piece, *Solfegietto*

FRANZ JOSEPH HAYDN (1732-1809) more than 50 *Sonatas*, themes and variations, *Concerto in D*

WOLFGANG AMADEUS MOZART (1756-1791) about 20 *Sonatas* (some unfinished) themes and variations, 27 piano concertos, chamber music with piano

LUDWIG VAN BEETHOVEN (1770-1827) 32 *Sonatas*, themes and variations, 5 piano concertos, chamber music with piano

NINETEENTH CENTURY (ROMANTIC ERA)

Beethoven could also be listed here, as he has changes of style. This period which is the "golden age" or heyday, of the piano, is noted for the character piece, which means a relatively short piece, often with a descriptive title. Traditional forms were much expanded

John Field (1782-1837) the first composer to write *Nocturnes*

FRANZ PETER SCHUBERT (1797-1828) his sonatas are much neglected because everyone is working on Beethoven's. Also wrote *Moments Musicaux, Impromptus*, the Trout Quintet and two piano trios

FELIX MENDELSSOHN (1809-1847) *Songs without Words, Children's Pieces, Caprices*, two piano concertos

FREDERIC CHOPIN (1810-1849) "the poet of the piano" who composed almost exclusively for the instrument: *Préludes, Etudes, Nocturnes, Ballades, Impromptus, Scherzi, Polonaises, Mazurkas*, two piano concertos

ROBERT SCHUMANN (1810-1856) sets of pieces with descriptive titles: *Kinderszenen, Waldszenen, Carnaval, Bunte Blätter, Papillons, Fantasiestücke, Romances, piano concerto in A minor*

Franz Liszt (1811-1886) *Années de Pelerinage*, Hungarian Rhapsodies, many etudes, two piano concertos

JOHANNES BRAHMS (1833-1897) Sets of short pieces: ballades, capriccios, intermezzi, rhapsodies, sonatas, themes and variations, waltzes, chamber music, two piano concertos
César Franck (1822-1890) *Prelude, Chorale, and Fugue*, short pieces
Gabriel Fauré (1845-1924) *Barcarolles, Impromptus, Nocturnes, Préludes*
Edvard Grieg (1843-1907) *Lyric Pieces*, piano concerto
Isaac Albeniz (1860-1909) *Iberia*
Edward MacDowell (1860-1908) *Woodland Sketches*, other sets of short pieces, piano concertos
Alexander Scriabin (1872-1915) many preludes in different sets, other short pieces, etudes, sonatas

IMPRESSIONISM
Entirely new and original harmonies, gorgeous sound
CLAUDE DEBUSSY (1862-1918) *Préludes* (2v) *Images, Estampes, Suite Bergamasque* (contains *Clair de Lune*) *Children's Corner, Pour le Piano, Etudes, L'Isle Joyeuse*
MAURICE RAVEL (1875-1937) *Pavane pour une infante défunte, Miroirs, Gaspard de la Nuit, Le Tombeau de Couperin*, two piano concertos, one for the left hand only

TWENTIETH CENTURY
There are far too many composers to give anything approximating a complete listing. Many of these composers are more well-known for their orchestral works. For the range of this book, I have concentrated on the first half of the century.
Erik Satie (1866-1925) many witty, short, satirical pieces, many with odd or humorous titles; three *Gymnopedies*
BÉLA BARTÓK (1881-1945) *Mikrokosmos* (6v) *Ten Easy Pieces, Sonatina*, three concertos
Igor Stravinsky (1882-1971) short teaching pieces, *Piano Rag Music*, four etudes, *Serenade en La, Sonata*
Heitor Villa-Lobos (1887-1959) The Baby's Dolls (includes *Punch*)
Jacques Ibert (1890-1962) Histoires
Sergei Prokofiev (1891-1953) *Music for Children*, op. 65, Sonatas, Toccata, various short pieces in a wide range of difficulty, five piano concertos
Darius Milhaud (1892-1974) *L'enfant aime, Accueil Amical, Saudades do Brazil*
Paul Hindemith (1895-1963) *Ludus Tonalis*

George Gershwin (1898-1937) Preludes, *Rhapsody in Blue, Concerto in F*
Francis Poulenc (1899-1963) *Mouvements Perpétuels, Pastourelle, Suite francaise,* nocturnes, many short pieces
Alexander Tcherepnin (1899-1977) Bagatelles
Aaron Copland (1900-1990) sonata, *Four Piano Blues, The Cat and the Mouse,* other short pieces
Aram Khachaturian (1903-1978) *Adventures of Ivan, Album for Young People, Toccata*, piano concerto
Dmitri Kabalevsky (1904-1987) many works for students (mentioned in text)
Dmitri Shostakovich (1906-1975) *Doll's Dances*, works for students, *24 Preludes and Fugues*
Olivier Messaien (1908-1972) *Préludes*

SAMPLE SYLLABUS OF REPERTOIRE

We are living in an age of transition regarding the publishing world. Bear in mind that you always want to have music that is clearly printed, large enough to see easily, in a reliable edition. Trusted editions are faithful to the composer's written notes, usually based on the authoritative editions of the complete works of a composer, with corrections where needed (yes, even the great composers made an occasional omission of a sharp, for instance), and editorial suggestions such as fingering and phrasing. You do not want an edition that is over-edited. For this reason, many teachers recommend Urtext editions. But even these can vary, as someone has to edit it. For a helpful explanation of the term Urtext, see the article by Harold Schonberg, in *The New York Times, What on Earth is an Urtext?* (March 24, 1974). Among publishers, Alfred has editions that are clearly printed, extremely well edited and reasonably priced. Dover offers good value in useful reprints. Other publishers of note include Peters, Schott, Boosey & Hawkes. Henle editions are beautiful and scholarly, but also pricey.

After you complete a basic beginner's method, you will be ready to proceed to original music. Your first purchases will most likely be a technique book (most teachers uses Hanon at this stage, and there are many editions available) a scale book, such as *Scales, Chords, Arpeggios and Cadences* (Palmer/Manus/Lethco) published by Alfred, or *The Brown Scale Book*, published by Frederick Harris. These will be permanent additions to your library, and you won't be using the whole volume at once.

For your repertoire,, the most expedient solution is an anthology, or collection of original material, such as the aforementioned *Easy Classics to Moderns* series edited by Denes Agay, or the *Essential Keyboard Repertoire* series edited by L. F. Olson. These volumes contain selections from Bach's *Notebook for Anna Magdalena Bach*, Leopold Mozart's *Notebook for Wolfgang*, selections from Schumann's *Album for the Young*, Bartók's *For Children*, Kabalevsky's op. 39 and op.27, and works by Prokofiev, Khachaturian, Stravinsky. All major composers who wrote works playable at this level are represented.

Scales, exercises, and arpeggios should be incorporated into regular practice. Quite a lot can be accomplished in five to ten minutes per practice session. When you have been away from the piano for awhile (traveling, for instance) it is a good idea to get back in shape with some exercises first. January and February are good months (where winters are severe) to begin a more concentrated effort. Vary the order that you practice scales (by order of Circle of Fifths, by fingering groups, major/minor).

The lists that follow are very general guidelines. You should always strive to learn at least a few compositions by any given composer. For one reason or another, a particular piece might not appeal, and it might not even be "typical" of the composer. Also, you should try to familiarize yourself with orchestral and chamber works of every composer you study. These lists are numbered I, II, III merely for convenience, as there are no official levels. Many easier pieces can still be (and should be) learned at a "higher" level, and a more difficult piece, if totally appealing, might be learned much sooner than expected. Eventually, you will be able to play many of these pieces at sight.

LITERATURE I:
The easiest selections from the aforementioned anthologies. Supplemental material from Bartók's *First Term at the Piano* and the first two volumes of *Mikrokosmos*. For those interested in 20th century music, *Kinderstücke* by Anton Webern is a good introduction to twelve tone writing, and there are many interesting pieces in Ross Lee Finney's *Piano Games*. A nodding acquaintance with the sounds will open the door to more appreciative listening of new works at concerts.

Once you have completed a fair amount of these pieces, you will be ready to move on to the more difficult works from Kabalevsky's op. 27, Prokofiev's op. 65, and begin a sonatina by Clementi or Kuhlau. The set of six sonatinas op. 36 by Clementi are good ones to try. They demonstrate the bare essentials of sonata form.

LITERATURE II:
Baroque Era:
Now you will want to purchase a copy of Bach's *Short Preludes*. An excellent edition is edited by Willard Palmer and published by Alfred.

A suggested beginning order might be the following (BWV numbers are given)
939 C major
924a C minor
999 C minor (originally for lute; Bach arranged this himself)
927 F major
935 D minor
926 D minor
929 G minor
924 C major
933 C major

Many (but not all) students enjoy C.P.E. Bach's *Solfeggietto*
Easier pieces by Couperin and Rameau

Domenico Scarlatti wrote over 550 "exercises" now called Sonatas, which will develop technique while practicing some lovely music (Kirkpatrick and Longo numbers are given in this suggested order)
D minor: K34, LS 7 (S means supplement)
D minor: K32, L423
G major: K431, L83
C major: K73b, L217
C minor: K11, L352
C minor: K40, L357
B-flat major: K440, L97
G major: K431, L83
G major: K391, L79

Ornamentation (embellishments, "grace notes" and trills) will be making appearances, especially in works of the baroque and classical periods. The subject can become as complicated and daunting as you wish, even a lifelong study, but it needn't become overwhelming or frightening. When you first read through a piece with ornamentation, leave out the ornamentation (as it might confuse the rhythm and obscure the main note). Then check if your edition suggests a "realization" (how to play the ornament), often in a footnote, or on an introductory page. Your music dictionary will also have information. Your teacher will guide you in learning the basic ornaments, trill, appoggiatura, acciaccatura, mordent, and turn. Do not lose sight or sound of the basic note that is being embellished. Trills in the baroque and classic eras generally begin on the note above, but this is not a hard and fast rule, you have to look at where the musical line is moving.

Classical Era:
After you have learned a few sonatinas, you will be ready to learn the Mozart Sonata K545 in C, the Haydn Sonata in C, usually listed as no. 35, and the Beethoven Sonata op. 49 no. 2 in G, then the op. 49 no. 1 in G minor. Now is the time to start learning about sonata form. For the actual music, your teacher can help you decide what to purchase; there is a good anthology of sonatas available from Alfred that contains all of the above. Other students many want to obtain the complete sonatas of each composer. It is always more economical to get the complete works, rather than individual sonatas, but your purchase should depend upon how much use of it you anticipate. Sonatas you are not ready to play yet can always be studied, as you would study a score.

Romantic Era:
More pieces from Schumann's op. 68, and also from *Kinderszenen*, op. 15.
There are not many pieces of Chopin at this level, but there are some short works in a collection from Alfred.
Mendelssohn's *Songs without Words*: the three Venetian Boat Songs are a good introduction.
Brahms, like Chopin, does not have much material at this level, but you could try the lovely *Waltz in A-flat*, op. 39 no. 15.

Impressionism
Debussy: *Album Leaf*, and *Jimbo's Lullaby* and *The Little Shepherd* from *Children's Corner* (this suite has titles in English, not French)
Ravel: *Prelude*

Twentieth Century
Prokofiev: *Music for Children*, op. 65: *Moon Strolls in the Meadows*, no. 12, *The Rain and the Rainbow*, no. 8 (the whole collection is delightful)
Bartok: *Ten Easy Pieces* (includes *Dawn* and *Evening in the Country*, and many interesting other pieces), *Mikrokosmos*, vol. 3
Copland: *Down a Country Lane* (a student favorite)

LITERATURE III

At this point, it is necessary to explain that any lists of levels, grades, categories, or ratings of piano music is at best arbitrary, moot, and variable. Do bear in mind also, that certain styles of composition, for example, Romantic music with bigger chords, are easier for some students who then might have trouble with contrapuntal lines.

As stated previously, good instruction and literature should be consistent for all beginning and intermediate students, no matter what their ages. That said, everyone does not have to learn exactly the same works, like a blueprint. There is ample choice available: no one should be forced to learn a disliked piece. The literature chosen should be real music, and not simplified versions of more difficult works. Once a student has progressed beyond the easiest sonatas by the classical era masters, and the two part inventions by Bach, age and aspirations should now be given serious consideration, as the emphasis and materials will now diverge.

For a talented youngster with ambition for a musical career, there will necessarily be more emphasis on technique, memorization, and theory, plus stricter adherence to curriculum requirements for admission to various institutions or competitions. Certain works are generally considered to be "too mature" for young people (some Beethoven sonatas, for example) but there is plenty of music remaining to be learned.

Students wishing to be an accompanist, or learning "secondary piano", aspiring music teachers for whom piano is not their main instrument, should be including a large amount of sight reading in their daily work, including the various forms as vocal scores, orchestral reductions, chamber music, and popular selections. These students should be encouraged to accompany other musicians whenever the opportunity arises.

An adult student who has a favorite composer or perhaps a category (musical comedy) will certainly want to include this extra material on the musical menu now.
How much to include on this menu? The balanced diet is the ideal, with some work from every stylistic period, including one longer work, most likely a sonata. But this would total four or five works, plus technique, sight reading, and review, so most of the time, this is not practical. It is useful to remember that several shorter works of a slightly easier level could be learned quickly, and add to the student's feeling of accomplishment, as well as increased knowledge of composers' works. Too many times, a student is assigned a long and arduous work (the teacher is understandably overjoyed to have someone able to study it) when several shorter works might have been mastered in the meantime.

For older students, I feel that exposure to as much literature as possible should be the goal. Piano study becomes a life-long pursuit, a journey, a study of the great composers. By playing the music, you are making a connection, something that mere listening cannot ever provide. Enrichment continues from broadening one's musical knowledge to include orchestral, chamber, and vocal works by a composer you are studying. The goal is to open the door to all this knowledge, and to keep growing and learning. Yes, it's OK to attempt a really great, difficult work. You are studying, and perfection is not necessary.

At this level of achievement, it is useful to have an anthology of reliable, "standard" classics. *Quiet Classics*, edited by Keith Snell, is a nice anthology to have handy.

Renaissance Composers.
Previously, there has not been enough time in music lessons to reach beyond the usual periods of study. For those who would like to explore the earlier music, there are the *Fitzwilliam Virginal Book* and *Parthenia*, for English composers, and there are collections of early Italian composers. Any collection of "old" music of this period would be useful for attuning the student's ear to the earlier harmonies.
Byrd, *The Lord of Salisbury's Pavan*
Frescobaldi, *La Frescobalda*

Baroque period
Bach, *Two part inventions*. A suggestion would be to begin with no. 13, then 1, 10, 14, 3. When enough two part inventions have been learned, it is time to move on to the *three part inventions*: a recommendation would be to start with no. 6 in E major. The F minor invention is a gem. From this point, there are the *French Suites*, then *The Well-Tempered Clavier* (a keystone for study), the *Partitas*, the *English Suites*, all material suitable for studies beyond the scope of this book.

Scarlatti sonatas:
"Pastorale" D minor, K9, L413
"Tempo di Ballo" D major, K430, L463
C major K159, L104
G major K2, L352
G major K431, L83
C minor K40, L57

F major K525, L188
F minor K481, L187
E major K380, L23
A major K322, L483
A minor K149, L93

French Baroque (take note of the descriptive titles)
Francois Couperin
Les barricades mysterieuses
Le Bavolet flottant
Soeur Monique
Louis-Claude Daquin
Le coucou
Jean-Philippe Rameau
Tambourin
La Poule
La Joyeuse

Classical era
At this point, the teacher should advise the student about the purchasing of complete editions, or a collection, such as the one edited by Maurice Hinson for Alfred.

Haydn
Hoboken numbers are given
D major #38 (very popular)
E minor #34
G major #40
G major #27

Mozart
Sonatas
G major K283
B flat major K570
E flat major K282
D major K311
B flat major K333
Fantasia in D minor K397

Beethoven
Sonatas
G major, op. 79
F minor, op. 2 no. 1
C minor, op. 10 no.1
F major, op. 10 no. 2
E major, op. 14 no. 1
"Moonlight" sonata, op. 27 no. 2, first movement
"Pathetique" sonata op. 13, second movement

Once the student has learned a selection of the above sonatas, there are many more to be studied and learned: the longer and greatest masterworks, which form the bedrock of the piano canon.

Nineteenth Century
John Field
Nocturnes (a good one to begin with is no. 5 in B-flat major)

Mendelssohn
Songs without Words
Op. 19, no. 1 in E major is especially lovely

Chopin
After the four shortest preludes are learned, the student can progress to op. 28 no. 15, the "*Raindrop*"
Nocturnes, op. 9 no.2, op. 15 no.3, op. 37 no.1, op. 55 no.1
Waltzes op. 34 no. 2, op. 64 nos. 1, 2, 3, op. 69 no.1, op.70 no.2
Mazurkas op. 7no.1,2 op. 33 no.3, op.67 nos.2, 3, 4, op. 68 no. 2

Schumann
Selections from *Kinderszenen*, op. 15

Brahms
Intermezzo in A minor, op. 76 no. 7
Intermezzo in A major op. 118 no. 2

Late nineteenth and twentieth century
MacDowell, Edward
To a Wild Rose from *Ten Woodland Sketches*, op. 51

Satie, Erik
Gymnopedies

Debussy
Dr. Gradus ad Parnassum (from *Children's Corner*)
Reverie
Clair de Lune (from *Suite Bergamasque*)
Deux Arabesques
Preludes, Book 1: *Danseuses de Delphes, La Fille aux cheveux de lin, La Cathedrale engloutie*

Gretchaninoff
Song of Autumn (no. 3 from *Pastels*, op. 3)

Ravel
Pavane pour une infante défunte

Villa-Lobos
Punch (*O Polichinello*) from *Prole do Bébé* (The Baby's Dolls) series 1

Ibert
A Giddy Girl (from *Histoires*)

Poulenc
Pastourelle (from *L'Eventail de Jeanne*)
Trois Mouvements perpetuels

Copland
In Evening Air
The Cat and the Mouse

SCALE PRACTICE

The complete list of scale fingerings, which follows, is given for reference. These fingerings are organized by fingering patterns, not by the Circle of Fifths.
A possible order is suggested (RH is right hand, LH is left hand):

Learn the C major pattern very well, as this is the basis for many scales. First learn hands separately. Then, it is useful to practice with the hands in contrary motion (start with two thumbs on Middle C). Start with one octave, then two, then work up to three. After you feel comfortable with the fingering, try hands together in parallel motion. If you get confused, go back to hands separately or contrary motion.

Next, the scales of G and D follow the same pattern. F major has a different RH pattern (no fifth finger is used) but the LH follows the C pattern.
Minor keys of A, E, D could be learned as well, as they follow the C pattern. The harmonic form of the minor is usually learned first.
The scales of A major and E major also follow the C pattern. E is especially good in contrary motion. It is said that Chopin taught pupils this scale first.
The scale of B major has a RH fingering like C major, but the LH has a pattern with no fifth finger used.

The scales of B flat and E flat major belong to a different fingering family, but once the pattern is understood, it is not difficult. Their relative minors of G and C follow the C major pattern.

The above list totals fourteen scales. As there are only twenty-four, you are more than halfway. The eventual goal would be to play them all, four octaves, but this skill is not necessary for the scope of this book. The fingering patterns are included for reference, and for those preparing for piano exams that require all the scales. The key point is to realize the fingering patterns, and which are the same.
It is a good idea to mark a Circle of Fifths with the scales as you learn them, to reinforce your knowledge of key signatures and relative minors. Along with the scale, you should also learn the tonic chord and the dominant chord of the key. Simple arpeggios can also be included here.

SCALE FINGERINGS

Capital letters are used for major keys, lower case for minor. Numbers are in ascending order; reverse for the descending

C, D, E, G, A
c, d, e, g, a
      RH 123-1234-123-1234-123-1234 (5 when ending)
      LH (5 when beginning) 4321-321-4321-321-4321-321
      The fingering is the same for both hands in contrary motion

B (and C-flat, its enharmonic: pitches are the same, spelling is different) and b
      RH C fingering
      LH 4321 4321

F, f   RH 1234 1234
      LH C fingering

E flat and B flat
      RH begins 2 1 2
      LH 321 4321

A flat and D flat (and C sharp, its enharmonic)
      RH begins 231
      LH 321 4321

e flat (and d sharp) RH begins 2 1   LH 214
b flat (and a sharp) RH begins 2 1   LH 213
a flat (and g sharp) RH begins 231   LH 3213

G flat and F sharp (these are enharmonics, and the keys are used approximately equally)
      RH begins 2341   LH begins 4321

f sharp   RH begins 231   LH 43213
c sharp   RH begins 231   LH 3214

CLASSICAL SONATA FORM

Classical sonata form is sometimes termed a procedure rather than a form. The term first movement form is also used, or sonata-allegro form. All the movements of a classical era sonata usually follow standard requirements, although there are some notable exceptions. These patterns are found not only in piano sonatas, but in chamber music (such as string quartets) concertos, and symphonies of the great masters, Haydn, Mozart, and Beethoven. The form is extended farther afield in the 19th century, but the thematic principles remain. Symphonies may have a slow introduction. Concertos have a double exposition (one for orchestra and one for the soloist) with no other repeat, and feature a cadenza for the soloist.

FIRST MOVEMENT (Sonata-allegro form) Fast tempo, usually allegro

<u>Exposition</u>

Main theme (stately quality)	Tonic key
Second theme (contrasting, more lyrical)	Dominant key
Closing theme or material	Dominant key

The exposition is then repeated

<u>Development</u>

Uses the material from the exposition, working through various keys back to the tonic key. (A notable exception is Beethoven's Symphony no. 3, the *Eroica*, which introduces a new theme in the development)

<u>Recapitulation</u>

Main theme, second theme, and closing material are all in the tonic key

SECOND MOVEMENT

For contrast, this is generally a slow movement, lyrical in quality, and some form of ABA or theme and variations, in a different key, most commonly the subdominant, dominant, or relative major.

THIRD MOVEMENT
Tonic key. If there are four movements, this will be a minuet and trio (the trio is a second minuet), or later on, as "upgraded" by Beethoven, a scherzo, which has a faster tempo. Symphonies and string quartets most often include this movement, as do some, but not all, sonatas.

FOURTH MOVEMENT
Tonic key. Normally a faster tempo than the more "stately" first movement, with a livelier, more playful theme. Often this movement is a <u>rondo</u>, which features a recurring main theme, or a combination form, the <u>sonata-rondo</u>, which contains more development as well as an exposition and recapitulation. This movement would be the third movement if the work has only three movements.

BOOK LIST

FOR STUDENTS

A music dictionary should be kept handy for quick reference. Two excellent ones:

Apel, Willi, and Ralph T. Daniel. *The Harvard Brief Dictionary of Music.*
New York: Washington Square Press, 1961 (many reprints)

Harnsberger, L. C. *Essential Dictionary of Music* [Van Nuys, CA] Alfred, 1996.

Copland, Aaron. *What to Listen for in Music.* [New York] Signet Classics, 2011.
Everyone interested in music should study this clearly written classic by a master composer and teacher (first published in 1939, and just as useful today). Highly recommended.

Nice to have: an illustrated history of music with pictures of the composers. There are some inexpensive volumes around, such as *The Great Composers*, by Wendy Thompson, which is also found as the second half of *Music: an illustrated encyclopedia*, by Max Wade Matthews and Wendy Thompson. [London] Lorenz Books, 2002.

Schonberg, Harold. *The Lives of the Great Composers*, 3rd ed. New York: Norton, 1997. A reliable and thorough reference, but there are not many illustrations.

Libbey, Ted. *The NPR Listener's Encyclopedia of Classical Music.* New York: Workman, 2006. A trove of information on composers, actual works of music, musical terms, and recommended recordings.

Note: there are many "guides" to recordings available, which are often the opinions of one or two people. There could be as many as twenty available recordings of certain works, so the writer's choice is personal and perhaps limited, not having heard all the recordings. It is important to listen to many different performances of an individual work, and not have one version or interpretation ingrained. Live concerts are always preferable to recordings.

FOR TEACHERS AND MUSIC MAJORS

Hinson, Maurice. *Guide to the Pianist's Repertoire*, 3rd ed. Bloomington, Indiana University Press, 2000. A thorough reference, organized alphabetically.

Magrath, Jane. *The Pianist's Guide to Standard Teaching Materials and Performance Literature.* [Van Nuys, CA] Alfred, 1995. Excellent, detailed reference for the earlier levels of study. Highly recommended.

Friskin, James, and Irwin Freundlich. *Music for the Piano.* New York: Dover, 1973. Still useful for its commentary and chronological organization.

Randel, Don Michael. *The Harvard Dictionary of Music,* 4th ed. Cambridge: Harvard University Press, 2003. The standard reference.

Grout, Donald Jay, and Claude V. Palisca. *A History of Western Music,* 5th ed. New York: Norton, 1996. This standard text has been through many editions, and there are music scores to accompany its study.

A reference to check information about composers, such as
Sadie, Stanley, ed. *The Norton/Grove Concise Encyclopedia of Music.* New York: Norton, 1988. For those who prefer the Internet, the complete *New Grove's Dictionary of Music and Musicians* is available on line.

BOOKS ABOUT THE PIANO

Fine, Larry. *The Piano Book,* 2nd ed. Boston: Brookside, 1990. Thorough treatment of everything you need to know regarding "buying & owning a new or used piano."

Gill, Dominic, ed. *The Book of the Piano.* Ithaca, NY: Cornell, 1981.

Isacoff, Stuart. *A Natural History of the Piano.* New York: Knopf, 2011. "The instrument, the music, and musicians, from Mozart to Modern Jazz, and everything in between."

The web site of Steinway & Sons contains much information.

ADDITIONAL SUGGESTIONS

Adams, Noah. *Piano Lessons: music, love & true adventure.* New York: Delacorte, 1996. A delightful, inspiring, and encouraging read.

Barron, James. *Piano: the making of a Steinway concert grand*. New York: Times Books, 2006.

Carhart, Thad. *The Piano Shop on the Left Bank*. New York: Random House, 2001. Another delightful read, and not just for musicians. You will painlessly learn much about pianos and their history.

Hafner, Katie. *A Romance on Three Legs: Glenn Gould's obsessive quest for the perfect piano*. [New York] Bloomsbury, 2008.

Kniess, Peri. *Grand Obsession: a piano odyssey*. New York: Scribner, 2008.

Lopez, Steve. *The Soloist*. New York: Berkley Books, 2008.
A book for everyone, later made into a movie.

Martin, Russell. *Beethoven's Hair*. New York: Broadway Books, 2000. "An extraordinary historical odyssey and a scientific mystery solved." Another book for the non-musician as well.

Powell, John. *How Music Works*. New York: Little, Brown, 2010. "The science and psychology of beautiful sounds, from Beethoven to the Beatles and beyond." Clear explanations by an author who is a physicist and a composer.

Rosen, Charles. *Piano Notes*. New York: The Free Press, 2002. Rewarding, with much useful information.

Schonberg, Harold C. *The Great Pianists*. Revised and updated. New York: Simon and Schuster, 1987. A classic reference, entertaining to read.

Siepmann, Jeremy. *The Piano*. New York: Knopf, 1997. Everyman's Library Music Companions.

Szpilman, Wladyslaw. *The Pianist: the extraordinary true story of one man's survival in Warsaw, 1939-1945*. New York: Picador, 1999. This important book should be read by everyone, not just musicians. The movie won Oscars for best actor, director, and adapted screenplay.

BEGINNING THEORY

The study of music theory begins with a single step, the **half-step** (also called the semitone). Measuring is done in half-steps. A half-step is the distance from one piano key to the very next one, white or black. The entire piano keyboard consists of 88 keys, each a half-step apart.

A **whole step** is the distance from one key to another with one key, black or white, in between. It equals two half-steps.

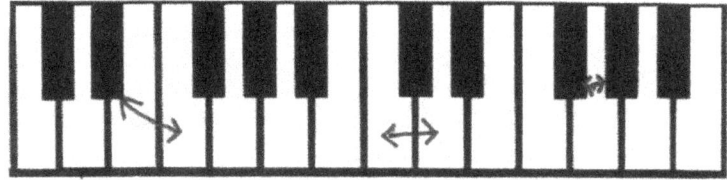

Written examples of half steps

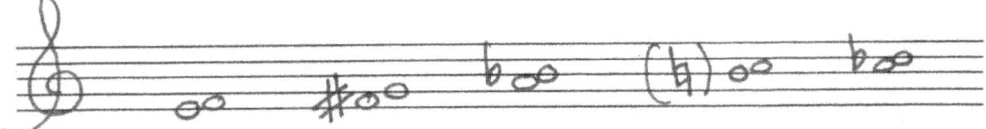

Written examples of whole steps

Play these and listen. What difference do you notice? These are also called intervals. An **interval** is defined as the space between two notes, and can be block ("solid") with the notes sounding together, or "broken" with the notes played separately.

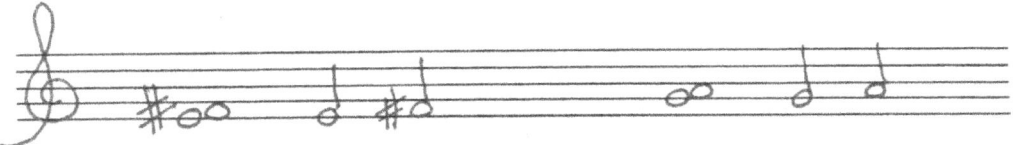

This interval is a **fifth**. It is a very important interval. Listen to the sound, sometimes described as "hollow" (think of string instruments tuning). The five finger exercises span a fifth. A fifth "measures" seven half steps in length. See if you can find all the fifths on the white keys.

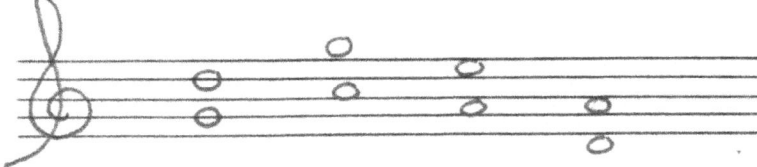

Here are all the intervals in order
M means major
m means minor
P means perfect, a term applied to prime, octave, fourth and fifth

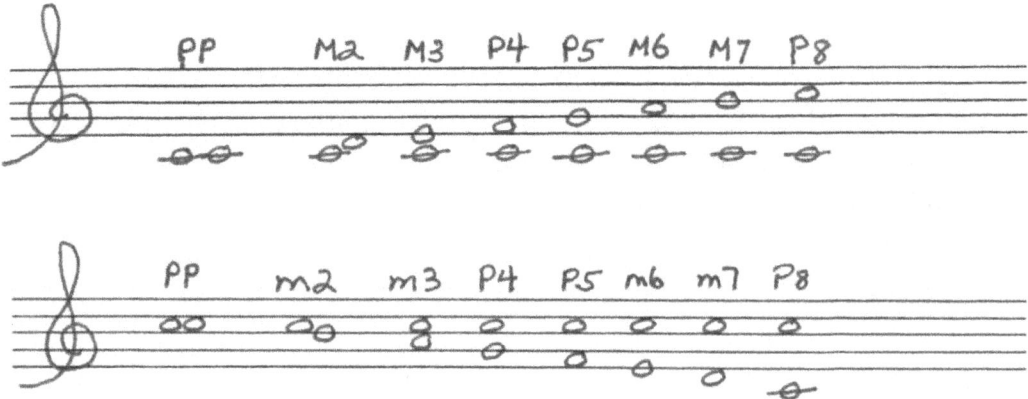

These are the intervals in their basic (unaltered) form. Do not be concerned about the terms perfect, major or minor at this time. Listen to the sound of each. Which are more dissonant? Intervals are the building blocks of chords and melody lines. Recognizing them will help your reading. This ability will eventually come together and be automatic. For puzzle lovers, intervals can be inverted: a 2nd becomes a 7th, and so on. Try to find some intervals in pieces you are learning.

TRIADS

A triad is a three note chord consisting of a root, a third, and a fifth.

Major triads are indicated by capital letters, in this case, C (or with capital Roman numerals when analyzing a passage)

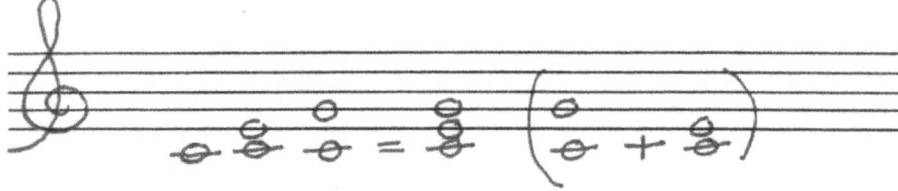

Minor triads are indicated by a lower case letter, in this case, c (or with lower case Roman numerals)

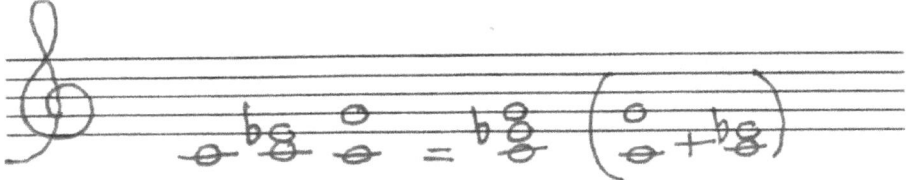

Play and listen to the difference in the sound. Note: hearing the interval of a fifth, with the sound "filled in" with the third is very important. The third makes the difference between a major and a minor triad. There is a method of teaching chords by piling thirds on top of each other. I find this counterproductive, and more difficult, especially with the larger chords, as the ear doesn't perceive the various thirds.

Triads consist of the three notes, root, third, and fifth, and can be block form (solid) or arpeggiated (broken). The root note of the chord is its name. A triad of C, a "C" chord, consists of C, E, G, and can have as many of these three notes as is possible, and it is still a C chord.

Remember that some of the greatest musical themes begin with "only" a simple triad (Beethoven's *Eroica*, Symphony no. 3)

The basic position of the triad is root position, with the root as the lowest note:

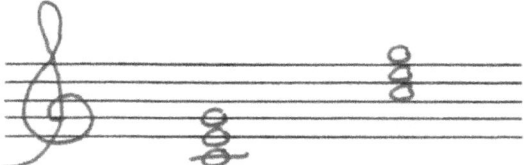

Triads can be **inverted** (first inversion and second inversion). Take off the bottom note, and place it on top, then do it again:

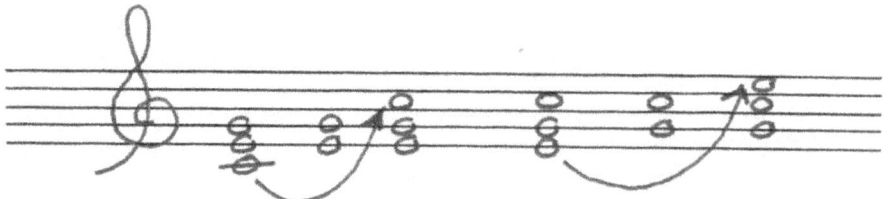

Observe what the bass note is, to determine what inversion the chord is in (note that the fifth of the chord is the bass note in the second inversion)

Arpeggios (broken chords) can be simple or elaborate, but they remain the same chord nevertheless (you can practice arpeggios in this pattern)

Triads can be changed ("altered") Don't forget to listen for the changes:
Major to Augmented (raise the 5th a half step) indicated by a plus sign

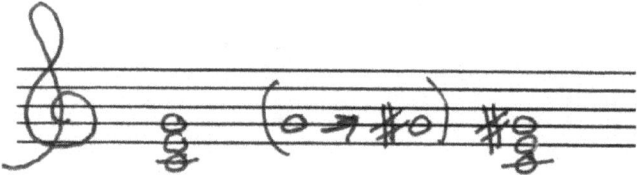

Minor to Diminished (lower the 5th a half step) indicated by a degree sign

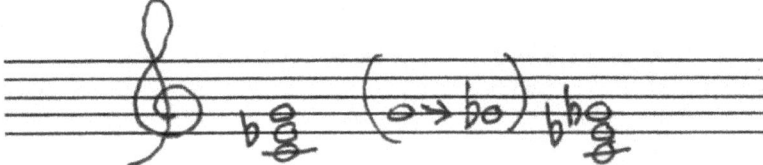

SCALES: MAJOR SCALES

There are hundreds of scales (a scale is an arrangement of linear notes, arranged by lowest to highest pitch, from *scala*, meaning ladder). In music theory of the periods we are studying, we are concerned mainly with two basic scales, major and minor. Scales are a very important part of musical composition. Much of the early study of theory is like learning the building blocks of grammar; everything will make sense eventually, but you do have to learn some fundamentals.

Major Scale pattern (half steps are marked with an arc) this pattern will work on any of the twelve notes
Scale of C

Scale of G (follow the pattern, beginning on G)

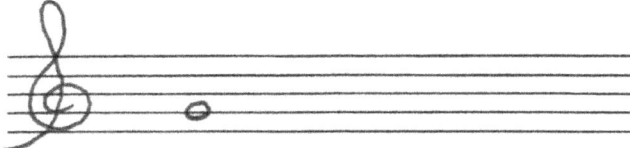

Scale of F (follow the pattern, beginning on F)

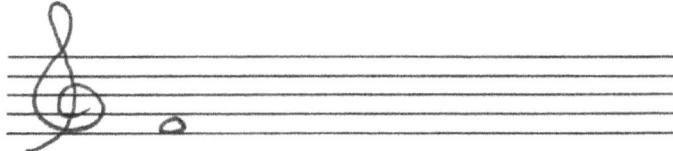

A scale must have a note for every letter name. The notes are sometimes referred to as *steps* or *degrees*. Always look for, and indicate, where half-steps occur. This is how the sharps or flats "get into" the scales, and thus form what is known as the *key signature*.

The key signature consists of the sharps or flats that are in the scale, and they are arranged in a specific order, which remains constant. One a sharp or flat is in the scale, it remains there, and the next one is added (the original small snowball is always present when you are making a snowman)

CIRCLE OF FIFTHS

Don't be intimidated: ease into this study. If you understand the principle behind it, you don't have to memorize anything. Start at the lowest C of the piano, and see how many 5th s in progression that you can find, moving upwards (try to do this by ear)

These are the starting notes of all the scales that have sharps (sharp scales)

Then start at the highest C of the piano and see how many 5th s you can find moving downwards

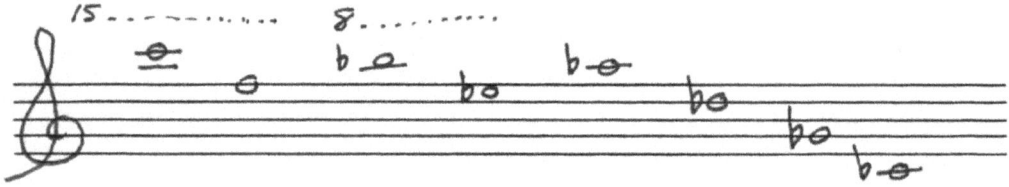

These are the starting notes of the scales that have flats (flat scales). Notice where there is duplication. These are enharmonic scales (pitch is the same, while the note "spelling" is different)

Everything about this circle works by 5th s (the order of the scales, both major and minor, and also the sharps and flats within the scales, called key signatures):

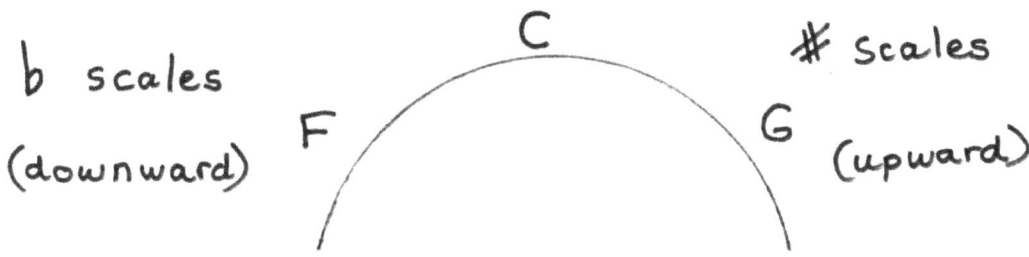

The "snowman" principle: once a sharp or flat is in a key signature, it stays in that position for all subsequent scales:

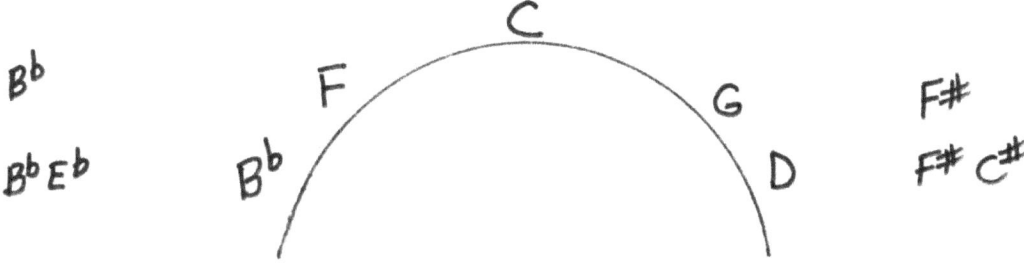

MORE ABOUT TRIADS

Triads can be built on every degree of the scale (they follow the key signature). Begin by writing out a major scale, and then writing the triad on each note:

Listen to the sounds: which are major chords, minor chords (one is diminished, can you hear the difference?) These chords will follow the same pattern in every key, I is major, ii is minor, etc.

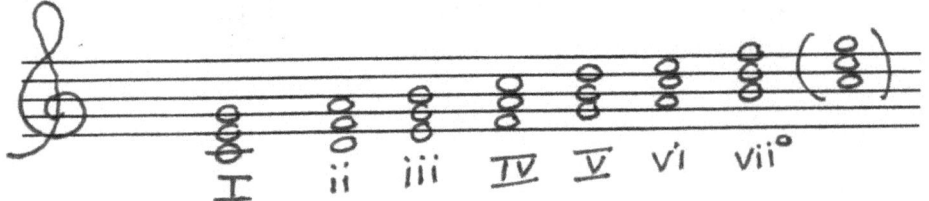

Capital Roman numerals indicate major, lower case, minor. This system is in widespread use. There is also a system of capital Roman numerals only, without identification of the type of chord. In popular music, the chord is identified by its actual letter name, such as "C" or "G" and is written above the staff.

Triads also have names. These are given for the sake of completeness; it is not necessary to memorize all the names immediately, though tonic and dominant should be learned.

Tonic (I)
Supertonic (ii)
Mediant (iii)
Subdominant (IV)
Dominant (V)
Submediant (vi)
Leading Tone (vii)

I, IV, and V are very important chords.
These are called the **primary triads.** The tonic is the tonal center, to which all the other chords move. The dominant, built on the fifth degree of the scale, is a very powerful chord and can engender much tension.

MINOR SCALES

Every major scale has a relative minor. As "relatives" they share a common key signature, which doesn't quite "fit" so there are some necessary adjustments.

The relative minor is found by counting down three half steps from the starting note of the major. This works out to be the sixth degree of the major scale, but the three half step method is much surer to employ, and avoids confusion.

There are three forms of the minor scale:

The **Natural Minor** follows the key signature exactly:

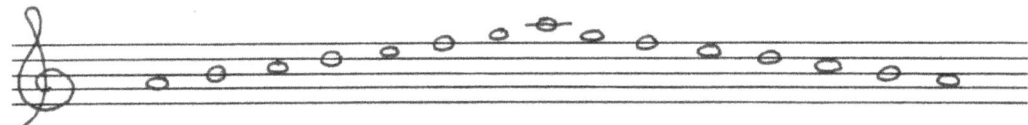

The **Harmonic Minor** raises the 7th degree ½ step, both ascending and descending (this is the most commonly practiced version)

The **Melodic Minor** raises both the 6th and 7th degrees when ascending, and follows the pattern of the natural minor for descending (this version is very necessary for certain harmonies)

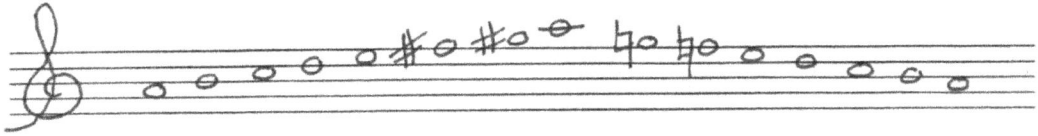

These alterations are never indicated in the key signature. The reason for all these variations is to have more notes to construct chords. The triads of the minor scale have more variations because of all these extra possibilities:

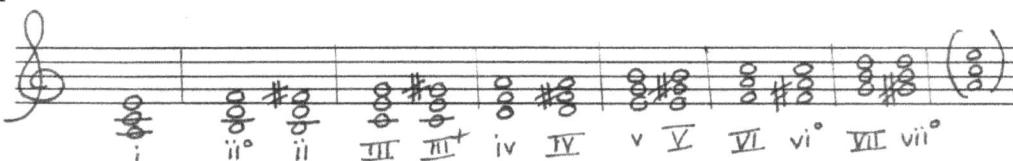

In Baroque music especially, you may find even the tonic chord adjusted, from a minor to a major chord (at the very end of the work). This is called a Picardy third.

There are twelve major and twelve minor scales, plus those that are written enharmonically, which means the pitches are the same, but the note spelling is different, for instance, the scales of F sharp major and G flat major.

To recap: the key signatures are derived from the notes of the scale. The music we are discussing will be major or minor. Different harmonic and compositional techniques are used from the early 20th century onwards, but many compositions will still have a tonal center.

You will want to be able to discern the differences between a major key and a minor key. The old chestnut that major keys are "happy" and minor keys are "sad", like most facile statements, is only partly true, but it is difficult indeed to find a good description of the differences. Minor keys are often thought of as somber and melancholy, but there are notable exceptions. Try to familiarize yourself with compositions in both major and minor keys. There are many Christmas carols that would serve as good examples of both.

Practice filling in a Circle of Fifths. You need a large circle, and enough space. Think of it as having a clock format, with C at twelve o'clock. The sharp keys begin with G at one o'clock, D at two o'clock, and so on. Each key is a fifth away from the previous one, and adds another sharp, which is a fifth away from the previous sharp. The flat keys move in the opposite direction, so F will be at eleven o'clock, B flat at ten o'clock, and the flats that are added are a fifth down from the previous one. The relative minor keys fit neatly inside the circle, and also move in fifths. Refer to a complete reference copy, for checking your answers.

Note: Your first attempts at writing clefs and notes will seem awkward, but after a few pages of scribbling, you get the hang of it quickly. Writing all these things down may seem cumbersome, but it is very important for learning. Students who write out key signatures, chords, and scales learn and retain far better than those who do not.

GETTING FAMILIAR WITH THE KEYS

Try to pick out a simple tune (by ear) in the key of C, such as Row, Row, Row your Boat. Then try to play the same tune on a different starting note, say G or F. This is called *transposition*.

Composers choose a particular key for a certain work, *why this key instead of that?* There are many possible explanations: composers usually "hear" what they want to "say" in a given key, chosen for its timbre, tones colors, range of notes, and even in the case of piano music, might try to emulate some other notes.

Remember that the five finger exercises (in the format that outlines the triad) when played in all keys can help you familiarize yourself with the chords in a painless manner. Arpeggio practice can do the same. Once learned, basic chords are never forgotten. A C chord is always a C chord (C, E, G). Its *function* can change if it is in a key other than C, but the notes remain the same. For instance, a C chord is the V (dominant) in the key of F, and the IV (subdominant) in the key of G.

Science lesson: overtones. Depress Middle C without making any sound. Then hit the low C (two octaves lower) and listen. What do you hear? Then do the same with depressing the E, G, B flat in turn, and hitting the same low C. The low note actually has all these other notes sounding along with it (these notes are called overtones) which is why music written in lower registers, whether for piano or orchestral instruments, is usually widely spaced for clarity of sound. Higher range notes do not have so many overtones. This is something to be aware of, especially when pedaling.

INTRODUCTION TO HARMONY

Most musical compositions you will play will either be a form of melody plus accompaniment, contrapuntal writing (where the musical lines, usually termed "voices" even though no one is singing, are equal in importance) or a combination of the two.

A simple example of contrapuntal writing is the canon, or round, which includes any songs that can be sung in that form, such *as Row, Row, Row Your Boat.*

Harmony is "there" even though there may be only one or two lines of music, and you can't "see" any solid chords. Composed music has a plan behind it; chords have a function, and don't simply float around in space. The musical movement of harmony is called chord progression. In traditional Western music, there is a tonal center around which the harmony revolves.

Simple progressions, of the primary chords (I, IV, and V) are generally found in scale books, usually entitled Cadences. These are very important chords, as they establish the tonal center, and recur constantly. It is a good idea to practice these in all keys, and, always keep listening. You want to get that V-I sound ingrained, and once you can hear it in other works, the world of harmony begins to make immediate sense. By being able to recognize these patterns, you begin to understand where a piece is "going" and you will play it more naturally, intelligently, and musically. You will know exactly where you are going, as in driving to a location you know well, as opposed to searching for an address.

A very common pattern of harmonic progression is the following:

iii – vi – IV (or ii) – V – I

You certainly don't have to analyze every piece you learn. As you progress, you will become familiar with certain recurring progressions (patterns of harmonic movement) and you will be able to figure out the harmony "behind" a piece that seems not to have enough notes for a chord. Do take note of any obvious chords in your pieces, including those in arpeggiated or Alberti bass form.

In all but the simplest of pieces, you will find *accidentals*. These are notes that are sharp, flat, or "natural" that are not indicated in the key signature. The basic seven triads of any key are akin to the Crayola box of eight crayons: for additional coloring and shading, you definitely need the box of sixty-four. Similarly in
music, for beauty and subtlety of harmony, you need additional chords, which are known *as altered chords*, or in other cases, the composer may *modulate* (move to another key). Sometimes there might be a change of key signature, in a longer work, but modulation most often occurs with only the accidentals written.

SEVENTH CHORDS: an introduction

Seventh chords are formed by adding the 7th above the main note of the triad (root). There are several different types of seventh chords, the **most common being the major-minor seventh, usually called the** *dominant seventh,* as it can be naturally built on the dominant of the scale.

This is a very powerful chord, as it demands resolution.
Try to find the dominant seventh in all keys. Start with a few at a time, so the task won't seem overwhelming.

Inversions: in any seventh chord, there are four notes, resulting in three inversions:

Another common seventh chord is the *full diminished seventh.* This chord is built on a diminished triad with a diminished seventh (always measured from the root of the chord) added. The good news is, there are actually only three full diminished seventh chords, as the others are enharmonic spellings or inversions:

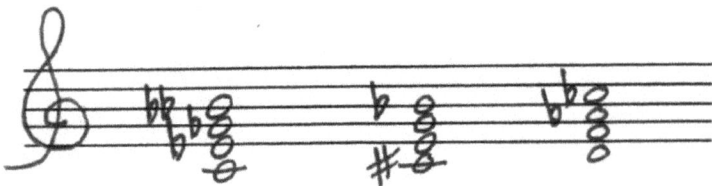

Again, listen for the tension in the chord. These chords are often "misspelled" i.e., written in an easier more "player-friendly" form, but any seventh chord should technically be written with the basic triad plus the seventh.

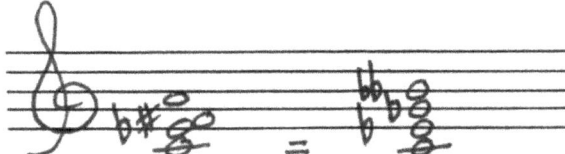

The **major seventh chord** is a major triad with a major seventh above the root. Remember the interval of the major seventh and how dissonant it sounded? Try listening to this chord, especially in a higher range:

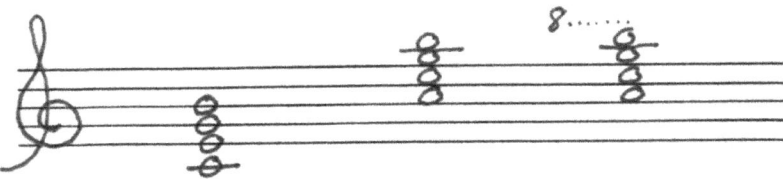

CIRCLE OF FIFTHS

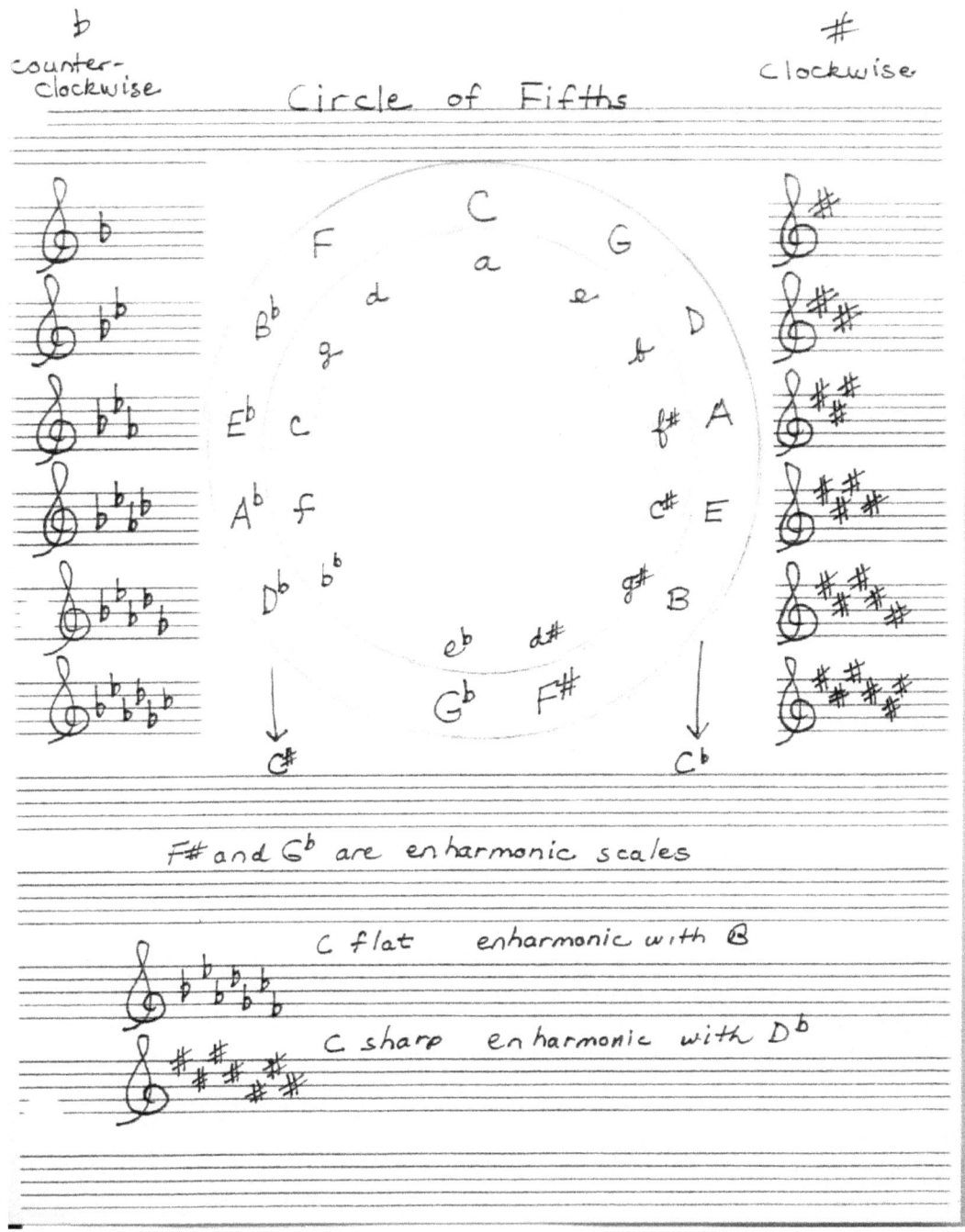

www.ingramcontent.com/pod-product-compliance
Lightning Source LLC
Chambersburg PA
CBHW081500040426
42446CB00016B/3327